Multiple Sclerosis

CAUSE

AND

EFFECT

How Stress Impacted My Thirty-Year Journey with Multiple Sclerosis

PETER J LICARI

Copyright © 2022 Peter J Licari

First Edition

Fulton Books
Meadville, PA

Published by Fulton Books 2022

ISBN 979-8-88505-067-8 (paperback)
ISBN 979-8-88505-068-5 (digital)

Printed in the United States of America

For Evan.

I am so proud of the man that you have become.
I love you, always and forever.

Special thanks to Monica.

Thank you for showing me what true happiness is and what real love can be once again! I love you!

To Vincent Spoto, Donna Aloi, Bob Maloney, Barbara Sachs-Traina, everyone with the MS Swimming Warriors at the JCC Wantagh, William McDonough, Tommy Morse, Shelly Osipoff, Frank Licari, Dennis Coen, and everyone in the Reaching for the Silver Lining support Group, and everyone in the Wantagh Support Group.

I Thank among others Bob McInnis.
northforkphoto.com

CONTENTS

Cathi, Will You Marry Me?

I WAS GOING OUT WITH Cathi exclusively for four years already, and I knew that I wanted to spend the rest of my life with her. I was happiest when I was with her, and we spent most waking hours together. I could be myself. She loved me, and I loved her. I didn't have to pretend I was anyone else! However, I feel that she always wanted the marriage to be sooner as opposed to later, but we both still wanted it. I have to admit, marriage was a scary thought though for me. None of my friends were married yet or even engaged yet, and I still felt that maybe I had more to do for myself. I don't think I was ready. However, I couldn't keep her waiting forever. "Hence, the engagement."

As silly as it was, I honestly thought that this engagement would buy me some time! I wasn't ready to grow up just yet, but…don't get me wrong, she was the girl for me! We laughed and made each other quite happy experiencing everything together. I was very sure that I wanted to spend the rest of my life with her. She was the very first thing I always thought of each morning and the last thing I thought about every night! I just didn't want to get married on *that* very day though! A long engagement would make me happy. Marriage was a big step and one that I know we both wanted, but it was just not for me that very moment!

We had spent a lot of time recently being controlled by jealousy, each of us, and it was getting worse instead of better. I honestly felt that once the ring was on her finger, it would take off a lot of stress for both of us, but mostly her. I was in no hurry to move forward, but I know she wanted to start a family. I honestly felt that I had the most beautiful girl on my arm both inside and out, and I never wanted anything more. But it was a love that might have come at the wrong time of life for me. I honestly felt that our engagement now would show her that I was serious enough to commit but still allow me to have more time to do what I wanted to do in my adolescence. I wasn't totally sold on this marriage at that time yet, but I knew she was. I did know that I wanted to spend the rest of my life with her though.

That was the problem! I still wanted to do everything in my power to do stuff that I always dreamed of doing, thought I could, and never miss a thing. I honestly thought that in my world, being married could not have taken place until I was ready and I had accomplished everything that I wanted. Marriage was not something that I wanted at that very moment. However, I always knew that she would be there for me and me for her. I had already figured out how I would ask her to marry me! I planned to organize a day this summer when we would go to the beach. I would secretly invite all our friends but not let any of them sit near us! I would hire a small plane that would drag a sign overhead on the beach that basically said, "CATHI, WILL YOU MARRY ME?"

"As it flew over, I would drop to one knee and ask her to marry me." Everyone that I had secretly invited—as many of our friends that could be there—would then come over to where we were hanging out and party! It would be this summer. I wanted it, and I really couldn't wait!

CHAPTER 1

Organizing a Band

I WAS DOING RESEARCH FOR my journalism class in early 1989 at SUNY Old Westbury to finish up my degree and get my diploma. I was a few credits shy of a bachelor's degree in business management, and I started to realize that I actually was just short of receiving a degree in journalism as a minor. In fact, I also had enough credits to get a minor in marketing also! Like a lot of people coming from high school, I was kind of lost in my desire for what I wanted to do in life. I had been grabbing courses that I had some interest in. Before I even realized it, I was working toward those minors, and I was only a few credits away from doing just that.

With my journalism interest, I figured that I could sort of use the system to help me with my minor. I had kept in contact with one of my friends who had started his own music magazine, so I gave him a call to see if he can help with my journalism minor. Frank, with the help of his brother, Gordon, had created and started a monthly music magazine called *Network*. The magazine focused on the local heavy metal music market on Long Island. Many years prior, Frank and I were on the same Little League team, and we became friends. In fact, he was actually invited to my thirteen-year-old birthday party! All through my years of playing Little League baseball, I was on his team, and his father was the coach. Then a few years later, having lost touch with each other in high school, we suddenly realized that we both had become little league managers of a group of twelve-year-old kids in the same Little League that we grew up in.

Looking across the diamond one day, Frank and Gordon were managers of their own team, and I was on the field, having become a manager myself of an opposing team. Looking like heavy metal rockers, they had both grown their hair really long, and because of this, they really fit right in with the kids.

Parents might consider them to be a little "different," but they were both really awesome role models for these kids! Their knowledge of baseball was incredible, and they both had a really good sense of humor which they shared with the kids. That is, they understood the kids greatly, and the kids felt extremely relaxed around them. The image of two young adults, each with long dangling black hair down to their waist, left parents of these children a little scared and concerned at first, but they all knew that those two would really educate the kids with patience and knowledge of the game. They made the kids feel special as well as they were both excellent coaches.

I approached Frank, and I just knew that he would do everything in his power to help me out with getting my diploma in journalism. As we were talking baseball surrounded by the yellow-and-green uniforms of our little league teams, the conversation came up that I was pursuing my journalism minor. I also added that I expressed an interest in seeing if they can use some help that would help me achieve my credit for journalism. Frank was all too eager to help me out, and I had to go to their house to help out with the layout for the magazine. As it turned out, it was just a formality that I "was helping out" as I really only did it just that one night. Frank had a lot of connections in the music business, and I was very interested in music. With him, I started putting out some feelers to get back into music. It seemed that Frank had a mutual acquaintance that was also putting out feelers to start a band and needed a bass player. Knowing that I played bass, he thought I should meet with him.

Very interested, I agreed with Frank and let him set a meeting up.

I was to meet with the guys Frank knew at a rehearsal studio called Flipside Studios in Huntington, Long Island, that Thursday night at seven thirty.

Tommy was that guy. He was dressed in dark-blue sweatpants and a cutoff white sweatshirt. He was a big guy in his twenties and had a full black beard that was trimmed neatly to his face. Tommy made me feel very comfortable right away in that he actually had a really good sense of humor and one that I would totally click with. He introduced me to Richie who was apparently the lead guitarist. Richie was wearing dark gray sweatpants, but they were speckled with streaks and spots of splattered various shades of paint. I guess he was some sort of a house painter or just an artist of some kind, but this allowed him to have a sloppy look about himself. He had long stringy brown hair, and that was loosely parted in the middle. Everything about him was covered with little specs of various colors of paint, and that was my opinion that totally gave off the rock vibe!

We conversed for a while as we gradually set up the room the way we were most comfortable. Tommy was the rhythm section with an acoustic electric guitar, set up to the far right. Richie was apparently the lead guitarist and set up in the middle. I was on bass and set up to the far left of the room. Tommy had a light royal blue Applause electric acoustic guitar that looked almost brand-new. Richie had a cream-colored Fender electric guitar that appeared to be well-used. Also, there was Mike whom I was told was the drummer. Mike wore a tight white muscle shirt with no sleeves, and my first impression was that there was no way that he was a true musician, but rather he looked sort of like he was a mechanic. A young Italian Guido-looking guy; if you don't know what I mean…straight out of a modern version of the movie *Saturday Night Fever* starring John Travolta.

I told them about my interests in music and what I liked to play. Both Richie and Tommy seemed to be very interested to hear my story about where I came from and what I was doing musically. Mike was just doodling around the drum set that was set up at the Flipside Studios. I told them about my history of being in a party band where I sang various songs, mostly progressive and commercial rock, including some Beatles, the Cars, and various Stray Cats songs.

The guys I hung out with were very much influenced heavily in the band Rush, playing their odd times and syncopated melodies, but none of us could do the vocals any real justice. Geddy Lee was the lead singer of Rush as well as the bass player, and nobody I knew could hit those notes as they were very high with any semblance of talent. I would often sing lead but had no real musical training other than sort of hitting the basic notes and struggling through the melody. Getty Lee, I felt, was an exceptional bassist and one that I tried very hard to emulate. Of course, I felt that I wasn't able to truly capture the ability but I held my own.

After some moments of trepidation, I jumped into Stray Cat Strut by the Stray Cats. As I did with the band that I often played with, "11:11," I grabbed the lead vocals. Even though I probably didn't have the best voice, I was never scared to grab the lead, and I wanted to show everyone there my ability.

"Black-and-orange stray cat sitting on the fence. He says meow…" (I purred like a cat.)

"Ain't got enough though to pay the rent…"

"I'm flat broke but I don't care…"

"I strut right by with my tail in the air."

We rattled through that song and several more hours of classic rock-and-roll songs, all with incredible energy that I have never felt. Within moments, I found out that the two of them both had more than adequate voices, and it was obvious that both felt very comfortable singing. They both sang great harmonies as well. I had never played in a band with such impressive vocals! In any band that I have ever played with, we just basically sang the songs just to keep the rhythm and allow some recognition of the song. We concentrated on the music and never so much on the vocals. However, in my eyes, this opened up a whole new chapter musically as both of these guys could really sing!

Richie had an amazing lead vocal and with such passion, and Tommy had an incredible ability to sing an incredible falsetto to complement Richie's vocals! Richie played a bluesy lead guitar, and he was able to give truly fascinating solos! He was a true musician. I had never played with as complete of a musician as Richie was. Tommy complemented him and gave it all a solid acoustic background. He fit right in with him and completed a full sound. Within the first few songs, I was able to realize that we indeed sounded pretty good together! I felt that they were representing a lot of different sounds as opposed to just the progressive rock sound where I had thrived from. As long as the music was decent, we considered vocals to be always second. Oh, sure we thought we could handle it, and as long as we sang the melody correctly, we felt we could get away with it.

However, listening to Tommy and Richie, I was able to see the truth. I felt that both of them had better-than-average voices. For the first time in my life, I felt like a child playing in an adult band. I had been in several bands that I thought were good, and we were, but each band had the same group of my childhood friends. I had a very small group of musical friends. What the songs and sound that these guys captured, I felt was incredible, and it showed that they were complete musicians!

Tommy played a better-than-average acoustic guitar, and Richie's solos were top-notch! Throw that in with better-than-average vocals, my bass playing, and I think we had a winning sound.

I was into a progressive rock sound in the vein of progressive music, such as Rush, Electric Light Orchestra, some Yes, and some of the band called the Police. However, I also had strong roots in the Beatles. Having grown up with a brother growing up in the sixties, like many others at that time, I was influenced by a lot of the music that my older brother liked. He would play on his turntable stuff I liked that I felt was not too strange, or sort of obscure, but was commercial so to speak. I always had an interest in music that allowed the bass guitar to play and write as a lead! It was in the vein of Paul McCartney, his musical proneness, or Geddy Lee's bass playing, and I wasn't happy with playing in the background with the melody driving the song. As shallow as it was, I wanted to stand out with my "chops" and show an obscure prowess for each song!

Often, I chose a harmonic or alternate sound to what was expected by most and allowed a flavorful twist to the melody as opposed to a driving beat. However, if a driving beat drove the song, I could do that also. As I said, I wanted to stand out and make the music grab my attention. Mind you, I felt I was not very good, but I felt that I was able to bring in an alternate sound than what was expected. I felt that I did have a knack to make a song catchy or different in that I am making it fun to play. I wanted to give some interest to the sound. I was very much into basically feeling that the bass should not be in the background so much. I wanted to be heard, felt, and add an element of something different to the sound. I felt that adding a little creative slice made the whole pie better!

Not only was Tommy into a very different style of music than I was; he was very happy not being the lead. He thrived on staying in the background to make the entire sound better and not stand out. I also felt he was much more into a romantic style of music. I never felt comfortable mentioning "love" or anything that was about love unless it was hidden with a play on words. My friends just wouldn't put up with that! In my eyes, Tommy wrote and listened to stuff that was very predictable, commercial, and almost sappy…not that there was anything wrong with that. I often compared him to some Chicago of the 1980s, even early Bryan Adams or Air Supply…etc. He was never shy about playing or writing about love, singing and saying all about it in no uncertain terms with no hidden meaning or agendas but just what he wanted to say. I would always find a way to say that same thing, but I liked hiding it so the listener could inter-pret their feelings without me actually saying exactly how I felt.

Growing up, I basically hung out with my friend, Carl; and our tastes were very influenced by each other and what we liked and listened to. The two of us never listened to that type of music, never mentioning love or feelings at all. But in the end, I still wanted to play music that was entertaining.

Out of everyone that I hung out with, I felt that Tommy was very comfortable in front of the microphone and had a better-than-aver-age voice. Then again, nobody that I had ever played with musically had any sort of substantial lead vocals. I told him many times that his voice always sounded like he had control of a falsetto, in that he had the amazing ability to sing perfect harmony to anything in the upper ranges. I never sang in a falsetto, choosing to rather strain my voice with the high notes! I was naive in assuming that nobody sang in a falsetto. Tommy did that effortlessly. He also had the ability to play a really solid rhythm guitar. I was never in a band that concentrated on vocals or music as much as Tommy did! He actually had a talent for that. He would write out all out on paper every cord change in easy-to-follow basic music format and structures of each song that we played. It was amazing! Whenever we got lost in a song, we would just ask Tommy to check his notes, and he would lead us back.

However, Tommy could not play the lead guitar. Some people were able to be creative in a lead role, but Tommy was perfectly happy supplying a very good rhythm. I think a really good and complete rhythm! I had also never played with the true lead guitarist, and I felt that was all that was missing for us to be a really special group! Don't get me wrong, I played with a lot of guitarists, and each one had its own ability. Each one had a certain repertoire of records, and they all held their own.

However, Richie came from a different idea of music than me and certainly Tommy. He was older by a few years than I was, and he was more mature musically. He backed it all with a killer lead guitar and a great voice. I guess my interest in music was considered progressive rock simply because of the crowd that I hung out with musically. I would definitely label Richie as having an earthy, bluesy vibe, but he knew his way around and was a well-rounded musician. He was able to basically fill the sound with classic and rather tasty guitar licks. I had never played with anyone as musically talented as he was.

However, he complemented Tommy and eventually me perfectly. He also had a great voice and was not afraid to take musical chances! By musical chances, I guess he was more into anything that sounded really musical but especially bluesy! He played music by Steve Ray Vaughn and then a few of the band called Oingo Boingo or some songs of various styles on the alternative side of music.

Some songs were very popular on the radio, but they had to be put into our own grove for us to play them. We changed some songs around to make it feel fresher and to our ability. For instance, we could not do a full horn section, and we never had a keyboard player to improvise, so we ad-libbed with various other sounds to get the feel for us. We played a few numbers by the band R.E.M and stuff that I would never have even considered playing, stuff with a different sound commercially and musically. Plus, he played the Beatles perfectly. Nailing the harmonies fantastically!

The two of them both opened my eyes to other sounds besides my music genre that I had enjoyed for years. For the first time musically, I was able to think that we could play any song well once we put our minds to it! Between the three of us, I felt that we could achieve anything musically. Tommy had a soft, commercial style, Richie was blues and alternative, and I was progressive rock in the vein of Rush, Electric Light Orchestra, and the Beatles. Kind of strange, but altogether, it all worked.

We were joined that night with another guy, Mike, who kept a beat but I felt was nothing spectacular. He kept good time, and that is all you wanted in a drummer. Of course, I was never very impressed with any other drummer having grown up with Carl, who was my friend since I was six and I felt was an amazing drummer. We clicked on so many levels musically that it was tough to play music with anyone else.

That first night in the studio was a learning experience for me. I was never afraid to step in front of the microphone, and these guys let me. I wanted to show the guys that I wasn't shy and that I was a force to be reckoned with…that I wasn't afraid to step in front of the microphone, and I started playing "Stray Cat Strut" (by the Stray Cats). Everyone joined in, and I was incredibly surprised at the full sound of everyone else in the band! Everyone jumped in; it sounded like we had been together for years! The sound was incredible. Tommy played an awesome rhythm guitar, and it was made that much more solid by Richie's lead guitar work! The sound was so full! I felt that there was nothing we couldn't do between the lead vocals, the harmonies, and the apparent drive of musicianship! What was great was the fact that these two guys could take the lead vocals and allow me to concentrate on the bass.

We met the following Tuesday night at Mike's parents' house in Massapequa. I packed up my 1982 Ibanez Road Star II off-white-colored bass into my 1973 sky blue Plymouth Duster. I had painted that car in various spots a dark primer gray to show people that I was working on it (even though I wasn't… I just *hated* the sky-blue paint job! I had no mechanical ability whatsoever to work on the car. A sky blue car was not a babe magnet at any age…but I thought that if I could just show that I was "working on it," that would be okay. I found my way to Mike's parent's house, and all of the cars parked in front of the house, I knew everybody was there ready. I didn't know what everybody else was driving but that had to be five cars there already.

For a good portion of the following year, Tommy, Richie, Mike, and I would meet in Mike's parents' basement in Massapequa to practice. It became a regular weekly event, and we actually got fairly decent.

CHAPTER 2

My First "Big Boy" Job

GROWING UP, THE THOUGHT OF working in retail was all I knew. I actually didn't have any direction about what I should do for a living. I knew I was going to be in the entertainment field, be it in performing music, writing, acting, or just plain doing something to be known, but I realize that I needed something to make money first. The only thing I knew was retail. I was a dreamer though, be it with my music or my writing. I even thought that I would do something on TV or radio—something creative because I was, after all, going to be famous!

In the meantime, however, retail was a decent occupation for me until I was discovered! I had been in retail since I was sixteen. Retail was the only job I ever had aside from delivering papers when I was in my early teens, so it was the only job I basically knew existed. I was good at it even though it really wasn't that difficult. All I had to do was be there for the customer, organize the merchandise, prepare the sales floor for merchandise, and interact with people, both internally and with the outside world. However, as time went on, I realize that it was not a very satisfying job for me both financially and creatively. Socially, it was amazing; I mean I made great friends, but that wouldn't make me famous!

However, upon my college graduation, I just assumed the next step would be in the corporate world. After taking five years to get my four-year degree for various reasons, I had graduated with a degree in business management and a minor in marketing and journalism. I chose to leave the retail environment for good and tried my luck in the corporate world.

I got what I considered to be my first corporate world job out of college the following summer after I had graduated in the spring of 1990. I was working within Caldor as a department manager of sporting goods while I was going to college to get my degree. While I was there, I had actually stumbled into something that was called a buyer or something in purchasing. That was simply by the fact that I was buying merchandise as needed for the company I work for within Caldor. I had fallen into working for a company within Caldor at a company known as Cresco, a merchandiser for the Caldor health and beauty department. In that position, I found myself in charge of ordering all the health and beauty supplies for a department at Caldor store number 102.

Caldor was a nationwide department store, and I had worked there for a few years as a sales associate in what was known as the seasonal department. There we sold all the seasonal merchandise, such as pool supplies and patio furniture in early spring to summer with Christmas and Hanukkah stuff in the winter. Frustrated with a lack of substantial pay, I spoke to management about an opening as a department manager for sporting goods. I had been filling in for that department occasionally anyway as it was located just a few aisles away from the seasonal department. The toy department separated the seasonal department from sporting goods on the left side of the building, and I was often there anyway to answer questions for customers in both departments.

Gradually, I asked, and I became the department manager of sporting goods simply because I was there anyway. I figured if I was doing work for that department anyway, why not get paid for it! Caldor management was eager to help, so I organize my school schedule so I would only have to go to school two days a week—Mondays and Wednesdays. They were long days for me, but I felt that it was worth it. I was finishing up my degree, so as long as I was able to work forty hours and still able to complete the necessary requirements for the job, they were happy to have me as the figurehead.

However, after more than a year and a half or so, I realized that it just wasn't worth it. That I felt was a life-changing moment for me was actually more of a stepping stone in my life.

I had become good friends with many of the people that worked at Cresco, which was working within Caldor. Cresco was an outside vendor that worked inside and for Caldor. At Cresco, I ordered, organized, and basically merchandised everything from feminine products to different over-the-counter medications to various candies in the department known as Fronts (which was cleverly called that, no doubt, because it was located at the front of the store). I was directly responsible for stocking the shelves of those products. I found out through very little investigation that in this position it was actually called a merchandiser.

As a merchandiser, I was actually filling the shelves with all sorts of merchandise that would be sold to the Caldor shopper but not actually work for Caldor. I would be working for Cresco. There was no haggling of pricing at all as it was still a retail store, but I was able to fill the shelves, so I convinced myself that it was actually a small form of buying or purchasing. I didn't have to negotiate pricing, but I had some interest in this. However, I soon realized that Cresco was not really a lifetime job for me but rather a stepping-stone.

After several months, I focused my attention on looking for a job that utilized the newfound skills and interests that I had obtained with Cresco. I realize that what I was doing was basically being a buyer, and I had an interest in that. I felt I was able to talk with people and could use my newfound skills of merchandising but needed to be taught basic negotiating; I think I would be good at that. I headed in that line of work.

After sending out several dozen résumés, I had several promising interviews. I was finally called in for a company called Multiline Technology that manufactured and produced several different machines that drilled holes in multilayer circuit boards. This was a booming business on Long Island and throughout the country. I sat with John, the manager of the purchasing department. I was immediately struck by John's size, and he apparently worked out a lot! He was immense! He had to be able to lift 300 pounds without even trying! We conversed about what the job would entail. This was a small company that was growing quickly and needed a member of the purchasing department to help with the company's growth if I was hired.

I thought that the interview went well, and I was apparently right. I was offered a position just a few days later. I was told to report at nine o'clock on May 29, 1989, and I showed up promptly at eight forty-five. I was wearing what I felt was my best suit: a dark-blue-colored suit accented with what I felt was a "corporate" yellow tie. The tie was highlighted with little navy-blue diamond shapes patterned throughout the fabric. I was introduced to Roderick who was apparently the overall department manager and was John's boss. Roderick was sporting a dirty blond Dutch-boy haircut and was wearing a sort of wrinkled white business shirt. It was all thrown together with a crooked solid red tie that barely hung over his apparent beer gut. Aside from John, Glen was the lone buyer in the department and was apparently the longest resident employee for the company. Along with Roderick, he had a sloppy look about him but also seemed like a nice guy.

I was told that Glen was going to be in an air traffic controller within a few months and was leaving the position shortly. Apparently, that's why I was hired so quickly to learn from him before he left. I was introduced to Donna. Donna, like many people I had met within the company thus far, was young in her early twenties. She had dirty brown shoulder-length curly hair and was dressed in casual business attire. Not that I am one to talk, but I was stuck with how incredibly thin she was.

I was shown around the hallway which contained three cubicles of the purchasing department on the left side and John's bigger office on the right side before we went walked to the right and down the hallway about twenty feet. As we approached a T in the hallway, we turned to the right where we walked past a small kitchen area on the left just before the bathrooms. There was a refrigerator and a water cooler on the left in that hallway also. We then opened a door onto a platform that led to a stairway downstairs. I was amazed just how big the place was once the door was opened up. It was nearly the size of a football field! There were more than several partitions that appeared to separate different departments and apparent workstations.

The headstock guy was this young kid named Lowell, who was I think Mexican or Puerto Rican for he was able to barely speak the English language. He spoke in a relatively high-pitched accent, which I found hysterical. He was a meek little guy who had to be no more than eighteen years old, I think, if that old! I was able to exchange polite greetings to a couple of guys on the floor as I was walking around with John as he introduced me. There was Darren who, upon my first impression, gave off a heavy metal rocker vibe with long wavy dirty blond David Lee Roth of Van Halen style hair. Then I was introduced to David, who was just walking by, and I was told was part of the inventory and control team. I was then led into the inventory and stock room where I met several women that apparently organized and ran that room. There was Debbie, who was the manager of that department with Laura and Tim.

Leaving the large manufacturing area and walking under the stairway, there was a door that we went through and that led to the accounting department as well as the sales department. I was introduced to Jim and Claire who were apparently part of the inside sales department. Just outside of that office was a hallway where two young girls named Colleen and Caroline were seated. They appeared to be about my age. I was told that among other things, they were handling all the UPS and FedEx for the company, both outgoing and incoming packages. To the right of Colleen's desk was a small window that opened up to the front desk and the front of the building.

After I was introduced to those two girls, John and I went through another door where there was a large desk where another young girl, Cindy the receptionist, was sitting. Cindy was apparently the company operator and was responsible for the switchboard and plant intercom as well as greeting guests. In front of Cindy was an open stairway of light oak that led up to the platform where to the right was a long dark wooden table and to the left was a door that opened back to the purchasing department. Just beyond the purchasing department and to the right was a small conference room that had a large picture window that overlooked the large work floor that we had just visited below. We walked down the hallway past where a small kitchen area was and stepped into the rest of the upstairs level, which was the engineering department.

In purchasing, cubicles were assigned as follows: Donna in the first four-by-six cubicle as you open the door into purchasing, and beyond that would be my four-by-six cubicle. Glen's cubicle followed next and then Roderick's office, which took up the remaining entire back wall of that department. Everyone was basically about the same age with the exception of the inside salespeople. Apparently, the company was going through a large growth spurt from what I can tell, and purchasing was to be a big part of growth.

On my first day, I was learning how to talk with different vendors supplying all the items that were written down on the various requisitions. My job was to purchase different materials that we needed for the lowest prices and all for the best delivery. I was to speak to different vendors to buy in general various sheet metals, various aluminum, and different electronic components for the machines that we built. All had to do with various specifications to use in the machines.

I was told when I was first hired that the only buyer there was Glen and John but that Glen would only be there for another three weeks or so while I learned the position. He was there as a buffer to the vendors for me and basically show me the ropes of what had to be done. Donna was one of the department expediters, and she also appeared to be very young with the rest of us.

I learned most of the purchasing aspect of the job or at least what was needed to satisfy that position and what was expected of me from everyone there. Within a few months at the job, Donna was diagnosed with Crohn's disease and had colitis. I had actually never heard of this illness. You would think that as a self-proclaimed hypochondriac, I would've known this, but I didn't!

One day, I had to go to the library to return a book for my mother, and so I picked up an encyclopedia and looked it up. Crohn's disease is an inflammatory bowel disease that affected any segment of the gastrointestinal tract. I had no idea.

She actually left the company soon after the announcement and was replaced by Debbie, a tiny girl with big curly brown hair. She had a very lively personality and fit right in with the entire purchasing group.

After Glenn left, they hired a guy by the name of Manny. Manny was born in Nigeria but had become a United States citizen a few years prior and was living in the country for about four years now. He spoke fairly good English, but he had a very distinct accent, so it was sometimes very difficult to understand him.

"Hi, this is Manny from Multiline…" He spoke in his deep, throaty accent.

"Manny"—usually followed by a short pause—"from Multiline?"

Apparently, the person on the other end of the phone couldn't understand him either.

This started just about every conversation at first until they recognized who this was.

Every day, the company needed various items from local distributors in that we needed to complete the production of the machine that was being built. Be it some sort of a spring or a bearing or even a piece of sheet metal that needed to be obtained quickly. That is why Multiline Technology had a company van that would pick up merchandise from local vendors to complete the project as needed.

Normally, every item that was needed for the machine to be built was ordered and was present before the machine could be built. Very often, however, an item was misplaced or broke before the machine could be completed. I was hired more than six months ago now, and the company driver for local pickups was this guy named Owen.

Owen was a college student who basically wore a white muscle undershirt and jeans ripped with holes throughout its tie-dyed color. That payday, he approached Roderick and told him he was putting in his notice, and now Multiline Technology would need a driver. Roderick made an announcement to everyone in purchasing, asking if anyone knew of someone that would be interested in doing that job. He said he would give $100 to the person if they could recommend and allow them to find a person to fit the requirement of a driver. I immediately thought of my best friend, Carl. Carl had not found his niche in life yet and was always looking for a job until he did. I felt that he would be perfect for this. Later that day, I gave Roderick his name, and he spoke to Carl. Carl came in for an interview the next day and was hired.

He would start work the following Monday! I would have my best friend working with me, and $100 in my pocket made it that much sweeter! Of course, I wouldn't tell him I got the 100 bucks until later, and I would use it the only way friends would, if you get what I mean!

The company vehicle was a dark navy-blue Ford 1981 van that was rusted in spots, but it had many thousands of miles on it. They were local miles as it was basically used to pick up any items locally that the company may have needed to finish a job, stuff like various-sized steel or aluminum plates for the machinery or any electronic component that we may have needed to get the job done. Carl fit in like a glove, and when he wasn't picking up merchandise for Multiline, he was able to spend time laughing with me like we did as kids.

As I said prior, I always felt that Carl was an above-average drummer, but he also had the amazing ability to find the little things that were so oddly timed or were in a repetitive pattern and find little idiosyncrasies that most people wouldn't hear. This, of course, would cause great pleasure and laughter once he was able to point it out. One example of this was that he told me that he was able to make that company van backfire at will by doing a certain number of repetitive procedures that he had discovered! Now, how he figured this out shows what kind of sick individual he was, but I found it to be pure genius. While traveling in the company van to pick up various items, he would often drive on the local parkways and maintain a certain speed.

After several miles and needing to release the gas pedal as was necessary with driving, the van would backfire, an incredibly loud explosion, almost like a gunshot! It didn't happen for a while, but a few days later, it happened again. Carl realized that after several tests, he found out that he could make this happen!

In fact, he could control it.

Well, that opened up is creative juices. In his infinite comedic wisdom and sheer driving determination to better entertain himself, he soon realized that he could make the van backfire after certain conditions to achieve this whenever he wanted! He thought that if he maintained the same speed of the van consistently and never altered that speed either faster or slower for an extended period of time, like a minute, and then quickly released his foot off the gas pedal, it would backfire! The longer he held the gas pedal before releasing the pedal, the louder it would be, and it would cause an ear-wrenching blast that was both startling and piercing, sounding like a rifle blast!

He told me that after some time and experimentation, he was able to control it to the point of only making it backfire at the exact time that he wanted it to! For example, if he saw that he was approaching an underpass on the highway, one where a backfire would be extra loud and echo in the underpass, having the van backfire at that moment was perfect! He would give himself bonus points if there was a pedestrian who was walking in the underpass! Watching a person jump out at their wits and cower just made the job that much better!

Only Carl could think of this, and that is why he is my best friend! We definitely share the same sense of sick, harmless humor.

One of the perks of this position was that every so often, a vendor would come in and give us various gifts, such as bottles of wine, various trinkets, and yearly calendars, or in a few cases, we were even given New York METS baseball tickets. I wasn't even a METS fan, but I went to several METS games, and the seats were incredible! This was all free according to Roderick; we were allowed to accept anything that would be considered a nominal gift. At Christmastime, many vendors would often bring stuff in for us all in the purchasing department. This was uncalled for, but I guess it was just business.

Over the few months that I was there already, I was able to see that Roderick was really very frugal with his money and especially liked to get things as inexpensively as possible. We all had to promise Roderick that anything we got from a vendor around holiday seasons, we would put in his office to be divvied up among all the buyers. That seemed very fair actually, but he would have the first pick of the bounty! It was especially exciting as many vendors would bring a gift—a bottle of wine or a small trinket—which I guess was a write-off for them, but we saw it as a perk for us.

The phones had a window on it that displayed who was calling and how long you were on each phone call. That was a standard. John would leave us alone to do what was needed. However, Roderick had a habit of sneaking up behind you. He would peer at the small green window monitor to see how long of a conversation you were having. If it wasn't Multiline Technology business and he needed something, you were in trouble. It's a little window that highlighted green letters and a built-in timer on the screen that had a running timer with how many seconds the phone call lasted.

Many times, Cathi would have an issue in our relationship and not like the conversation that I was having.

"No, I can't do that right now." I would tell her, and she would call a couple of seconds later, each time having to go through Cindy, the receptionist, to get to me. More than once, I actually told Cindy not to connect the phone call from Cathi if she called back.

"I am at work!" I would plead to Cathi in a stern but controlled whisper, but apparently, she didn't quite understand. She would argue and fight to the point of me just hanging up the phone on her. I was in the place of business, and at least once a week, I would have to tell Cindy not to let her call through as I was working. I'm sure it was not what Cathi wanted to hear, but at this point, it was my livelihood, and it had to be done! More than once, Roderick actually walked up behind me and looked at the screen on my phone just to see how long I was on the phone. I was not doing company business, and he would get upset! I could not blame him!

I would finish my job that afternoon, go home or to Cathi's house, and finish the conversation that she felt was imperative to talk about at that moment. Chances were cooler heads would prevail in the conversation; it would be short-lived. Cathi had a *very* jealous streak in her, and I didn't think there was anything I could do to stop that. In fact, *every* argument that we had was based on jealousy, which started out with only her and but gradually changed over to me.

At first, I was very content with the situation, but gradually over the years that we had been together, we seemed to be exploiting our insecurities. From what I could see, we both should have had none, but there it was. Cathi, I felt, grew into an exceptionally attractive person physically and with a great personality, and I was lucky to have her in my life. That is not to say that she was unattractive when we first started dating, but I felt that she really blossomed! I couldn't believe that she was with me, but in a lot of ways, I think I took advantage of that and her love for me. I just felt in my heart that she would always be there for me, I would be for her, and I guess I almost took advantage of that.

I would go on break with most people in the company at ten o'clock every day when the coffee truck would pull into the parking lot. This was the time that those in the company when most people took a fifteen-minute break. At this time, much of the staff would meet in the break room and just converse. Everyone there would look forward to hanging out for that fifteen-minute break each and every day! It was all just basic conversation, but I started looking forward to talking a lot to that girl downstairs, Colleen as well as others but especially Colleen. I don't know, there was something about her. I was attracted to her and felt that was a really nice person, one that I would like to hang out with more *if* I was given half the opportunity and *if* I wasn't in a relationship already.

I actually broached the subject with her to see if she wanted to hang out sometime or maybe want to see my band. That was my way to maybe grab the attention of the conversation with any girl. Darren was also there, and music was, I thought, a great way to get closer to Colleen at least in conversation. Darren looked the part of the heavy rock-and-roll singer, you know, with the long curly blonde hair. Kind of like a David Lee Roth of Van Halen look. I admit I was kind of jealous of him and wanted to do what I could to get Colleen's attention from him. I would call her sometimes just to verify that she was going to be available for a break for absolutely no reason other than to do it. Sometimes, I had to leave a message, and she would call me back. I have to admit that when my phone rang in my cubicle and I saw the incoming call on my phone extension was number 138, like a schoolboy who just received a note on my desk, my heart skipped a beat.

As I had said before, I would never cheat on Cathi. In fact, I have *never* cheated on anyone *ever*, but I guess it was my way of feeling good about myself. I mean who doesn't want to fantasize? I think that we all need that as long as it doesn't go any further. Being in a relationship for four years with Cathi though, the longest I have ever been in a relationship with someone and never thinking of anyone else, I guess I just wanted to see if others still found me attractive. I was thinking about asking Cathi to marry me in a few months, so I wanted to be sure! I think that it is human nature to actually see someone attractive and wonder…to *not* be intimidated by them and see if you still "got it." I thought that this was totally understandable as long as it doesn't go any further, and it never would.

Was that so wrong? I had no interest in leaving Cathi ever, but I didn't think it was so wrong to befriend whom I was attracted to.

CHAPTER 3

Tuesday Night-Band Night

FOR A GOOD PORTION OF the following year, Tommy, Richie, Mike, and I would meet in Mike's parents' basement in Massapequa, Long Island, for band practice. It actually became a regular weekly event for us. We played what I felt was a really good party list of songs, including "What I Like About You" and "Love Me to the Max" by the Romantics, "Good Loving" by the Rascals, "Good Girls Don't" by the Knack, "Rock this Town" and "Stray Cat Strut" by the Stray Cats, among other songs and by various bands. Of course, there were a few of the Beatles' songs, such as "Twist and Shout" and "I Saw Her Standing There." I especially liked "I Saw Her Standing There" as I guess it allowed me to overplay the baseline. I wanted to play what I heard, and sometimes, it was more than what was there. Sometimes, what I heard was a simplistic version of the actual song, and I always overplayed the baseline a bit, but that was the way I always heard it and ultimately liked it. I wanted to play the song so people could hear it, but I wanted to make it enjoyable for me and my baseline.

All this time, we were actually getting to know each other, and I felt like playing some really good music. Although I felt that we had really good vocals, there was a certain bit of another sound we each wanted to explore. Tommy broached the subject of us possibly getting one of his friends that he knew of who had really good vocals. After a brief conversation, we agreed to give Tommy's friend a try. I didn't care, and if he was as good as Tommy said he was, what could it hurt?

Conrad was a perfect front man, and I felt had an amazing voice! He sounded a lot like Steve Perry of the rock band Journey! I didn't know of anybody who could do that, at least not consistently. All my friends were just singers second, relying on their instruments to be first, but that was Conrad's instrument. He often said that because he didn't play any musical instruments that you can see, he felt that his voice was in the instrument. I did feel that he was an exceptional talent.

His vocals would definitely put us in another league! An added bonus was that he appeared to be a decent guy! He had looks, had a great sense of humor, and fit right in with us, all of which as you can see was very important to me. He fit right in with us all the very first time we met, and I felt that now there wasn't a song that we couldn't play! His vocals opened up so many more doors for me because now there was no such thing as we couldn't play the song because nobody could sing it. We had what I feel was amazing vocals, a great rhythm section, fantastic harmonies, and an awesome guitarist! An added bonus was that we all got along.

The only problem that I saw, and it really wasn't a problem if we used it right, was that we all came from different musical backgrounds. That is, we all leaned heavily on various styles of music that we each found very intriguing but didn't necessarily exclusively listen to it. While we each respected and tolerated each other music, we each definitely leaned to the sounds that each one liked. As I've said before, I like music that was heavily influenced with a driving bass that stood out, which actually makes sense as I am a bass player. Richie leaned heavily into a bluesy sound, but he also liked offbeat stuff, such as Oingo Boingo and what I would consider some really alternative sounds. I had never had any interest in any other music besides what my inner circle listened to: Rush, the Beatles, Electric Light Orchestra, and some various other stuff. Tommy was not really into anything that I enjoyed, but I admit if it sounded good, he wouldn't stop us from playing it. However, I do have to admit that I felt that he had a preset notion of what music should be played at a party and didn't stray from that too often. I thought Tommy was into what I felt was a more commercial, mellow, sappy sound such as later Chicago or even some Air Supply. Now with Conrad in the mix, we could learn most Journey to utilize his talents and not miss a beat!

We also did some stuff more commercial, like Joan Jett's "I Hate Myself for Loving You" to Billy Idol's "White Wedding" and any sound in between. That was a much more commercially acceptable sound anyway and really utilized our individual talents! Put that all together, and in an odd way, it worked out awesome!

As I said, I thought Conrad had a really great voice or at least one that I never heard locally before. He did sound like Steve Perry of the rock band Journey, and he was spot on! His vocals really put us in another league as far as a band. Many bands sounded good, but they were missing certain components. Some had a killer lead guitarist, some had great vocals, some were able to play songs that really riled up the crowd, and some seem to have it all. If we couldn't make the song sound better than the original, then we ended up putting our own spin on the song. I honestly felt that this situation was more of a borderline complete package. As I said before, I had never even have dreamed of being in a band this good! It also worked out that he fit right in! We were all around the same age, and we all had the same sense of humor. Conrad did things that made me laugh…hard!

We played a couple of shows with Mike on drums, but after a while, that sort of broke up. It was for no actual reason though, other than the fact that we all have our own lives, and each time we did show, we took several months off to handle various things. I know in my case I couldn't really concentrate as I had other things going on in my life. Between my school work, my job (I was a manager of sporting goods in Caldor), I was a Little League manager for thirteen-year-old kids in my hometown, my relationship with Cathi, and I wanted to have a social life, I was very busy. But if something came up that I wanted to do, I would make time somehow!

Tommy was working in a Rock Bottom in Wantagh, Long Island, and he had gone into the Sequa Deli right next door to get his lunch every so often. One afternoon, he spoke with John who worked there, and after several conversations, they realize that they had a lot in common. Both were really into music and wanted to entertain people. John actually played drums, which Tommy was always looking for musicians to play with and had been looking for a new drummer since we had split up with Mike from Massapequa. During the conversation, Tommy offered John to meet us one night in the studio. That was actually a very big chance that Tommy took, but it all worked out great!

We ended up going to a place to practice called Long Island Rocks. This was a rehearsal studio where local bands would practice off Sunrise Highway in Massapequa. It was right across Sunrise Highway from what was known as the Massapequa Mall and located in an industrial area. We were there every Tuesday at seven thirty for a few months. We would play a various array of songs that we had discussed prior, and it was our individual jobs to learn our respective parts. Tommy supplied us each with cassette tapes which had a version of each song if needed. He was awesome that way! He spent a lot of time doing that for each of us when we needed it and got pretty annoyed when we didn't learn the parts. Actually, I should say when "I" didn't learn my part as I had a knack for not learning it until I was sure we were playing it. I chose rather to just ad-lib most of the songs, which caused some friction between Tommy and me, but I really didn't like to practice too much. I just had too many other things to do in my life I wanted to do instead of practicing other people's songs. I honestly felt that once I got the song down in my head, regardless if it was played right or wrong, I felt I could just ad-lib it until I got it right.

```
 1   TWIST -N- SHOUT
 2   I SAW HER STANDING THERE
 3   FRUSTRATED
 4   ~~REMEMBER~~ GOT ME WHERE YOU WANTED
 5   WHAT I LIKE ABOUT YOU
 6   SLOW DOWN                            (TOM)
 7   GOOD LOVIN
✓    TWO PRINCES
✓    ROCK THIS TOWN
     LOVE SHACK                          TOM
     ~~PAPER~~ + FIRE
✓    LONG TRAIN RUNNING
✓    WALKING ON SUNSHINE
✓ ✓  ALL I WANT
     ITS THE END OF THE WORLD
     LOVE ME TO THE MAX
     ROCK AROUND THE CLOCK, HOUND DOG.
✓    CAN'T BUY ME LOVE
     RESPECT
     HEAT WAVE
     1 23 / ABC   MEDLEY
✓    YOU MAY RIGHT
     HELP
     MOODS FOR MODERN
     SWING TOWN
     PUMP IT UP
```

CHAPTER 4

My Inner Circle

I WAS EXTREMELY FORTUNATE IN my life that I had an amazing assortment of close friends. (Of course, I can never tell them that!) There was Carl whom I had grown up with and known since I was six and was what I would consider my best friend. He only lived at the top of my block, so we hung out all the time. Carl was what I felt was an exceptional drummer, and I was a bass player with vocal capabilities. We enjoyed the same type of music, the same type of comedy, and the same type of anything fun. We both had a unique ability to make each other laugh at stupid things. Then there was Mike, Burt, and John, all of whom I had met in Caldor. There was Bob whom I had met through John as John had gone to school with him, and they had become friends. Always looking for something to do after the interruption known as work, Carl, John, Mike, Burt, and I thought it would be really great to hang out and play cards. Of course, drinking some beers and the usual verbal abuse of each other was also on the menu! John said he would invite his friend, Bob, along so we would have five guys to play cards.

The date was set for the following Friday night where we all merged to John's parents' house in West Babylon, New York. One by one, we showed up and climbed down the flight of steps to the finished basement. Down there was a large banquet table, couch, a TV, connecting to another room was a bathroom, and, of course, a bar which had a refrigerator which was now stocked with various assortments of bottled beer. It started out with the usual adolescent favorites of Coors Light or Budweiser, but as our tastes developed, so did our palette! Corona, the Mexican beer favorite, was often served with or without a lime. Of course, Sam Adams was a favorite of all of us, but we jumped around with basically what was on sale that week. We each had our favorites, but our opinions were swayed with whatever was on sale that week.

John's parents slept two floors upstairs in the high ranch in West Babylon, so we could make as much noise as we wanted to! Each week, we all look forward to hanging out, playing cards, and verbally abusing each other! That became our weekly get-together, playing nickel, dime, and quarter poker, as well as several variations of poker-like games.

Of course, various styles of bottled beer and flatulence ensued! We played both five-card and seven-card stud poker, both standard and draw. With standard, you were given five cards, and you had to make the best hand out of those five cards. You would get no additional cards to make a better hand. With the draw, you are allowed to pick the best to two cards if you wanted and throw back up to three cards to the dealer unless you had an ace in your hand then and only then can you get rid of four cards, but that told everyone at the table that you had a poor hand and that you were going to start over.

Occasionally, a dealer would announce to all the players to pass a card to the left or the right, which would really mess up the odds of a player, either good or bad! Each time you drew, there was a round of betting. Usually, it was no more than a quarter for each bet unless you want to be verbally assaulted by the other players. Sometimes, we played a game called "Follow the Queen," which was dealt all seven cards facedown to each player. You are given seven cards, but as each player turned them over one at a time, you're able to see your hand slowly grow, stopping only when you have the best hand on the table. As the dealer turns the next card or cards over until your hand that was showing was beat. All the while if the queen turns up, the next card would be wild for the table and, thus, changing all the hands involved. We played a game called "Roll Your Own," which Burt actually called Taco Bell for absolutely no reason whatsoever other than the fact that he apparently couldn't remember the name and it stuck.

"Taco Bell," Burt said as he dealt out the cards.

In that game, you will gradually deal five cards, one at a time, followed by a round of betting. You would make the best hand that you could. The low whole card in your hand was wild, so that meant that every hand had a pair. But that also meant that technically you could have a great hand dealt to you until the last card and be dealt a lower card for the last card. That would mess everything up for you.

We also played a game called *Guts*! That was a game that everyone really liked because nickel, dime, quarter games would not include a lot of money. But with *Guts*, I've seen the pot reach $29! It was played much like Acey Deucey, which was a game that you were given two cards and you had at that the third card would be in the middle of the spread. For example, if you were given a three in any face (meaning suit, such as club, dime, heart, or spade) and the next card was a ten of any face and it became your anchor card, you had to bet that next card would be in the middle in the value. In this case, it was a four, five, six, seven, eight, or nine of any face. If you were dealt a card that fell in the middle, you would win that hand! Obviously, if you were dealt a card that wasn't in the middle, you lost. But the fun was if you matched one of the anchor cards, in this case a three or a ten. If you matched the anchor, you had to *double the pot*!

Now throw in a wild card into the mix, such as one of the one-eyed jacks, either the jack of hearts or the jack of spades, simply called that because there is one face on the card. The suicide king may be called "wild" in some games, and that is the king of hearts and it's called that because his sword is through his head, or a random card can be used. That would have messed up all the odds and made the game that much more challenging. There is nothing more humiliating than to have a great hand with a large pot which you are sure to win with the cards you're dealt and having wild cards mess up the odds and you lose! That was definitely followed by earth-shattering howls, screams, fist pounding, and laughter by your "friends" at the table as it meant the game would continue and you would have to count your coins to pay your debt.

If you matched the anchor and had to double the pot, it was enough to wipe your winnings out for the evening or even put you in debt for the evening! Many times. I had to send the check to cover my losses of which the checks were photocopied and placed in plain sight to remind me of my losses.

We had all worked together in Caldor and had become really good friends. Occasionally, Cathi and I even went on several dates with most of the same group. Carl was dating Theresa, whom they had met as one of my sales employees that I was in charge of when I was a manager of sporting goods at Caldor, Burt was dating Melissa, and Mike was dating Marie. Melissa was a cute young girl that I have to admit I was kind of attracted to, but I wouldn't even attempt to do anything as I was in a relationship with Cathi. I really loved Cathi very much. Besides, Melissa was a couple of years younger than I was, and I guess I was actually pretty happy that Burt had started dating her. Burt had a beautiful brand-new cherry apple red Toyota 4Runner that was the envy of us all I felt. His father was a bigwig in some company, and I think he had bought the car for Burt, but we really didn't care! There was plenty of room in the vehicle to hang out, and this would definitely allow us all to hang out together.

Burt's parents had a house upstate that Bob, Carl, John, Mike, one of Mike's friends, Rob, and I went up one winter to just hang out. This winter was just in time to go upstate and hang out with my friends! Of course, I could've gone away with Cathi, but none of the other guys were taking their girlfriends. This would be a two-day get-away up to Burt's house where we can just all hang out, drink cheap beer, film silly skits on a VCR camcorder, play 'nickel/dime/quarter poker' and play some Dungeons & Dragons.

Dungeons & Dragons, better known as D&D by us "sophisti-cated nerds," is a tabletop, role-playing fantasy game. It was played as you and your friends would sit around the table and pretend that we were heroes and we would go on epic adventures together to faraway lands, castles, and fight mythical creatures with magic and swords.

This would technically be playing in your imagination but once controlled by various roles of strangely shaped dice. There were eight dice, and they were all of different shapes and denominations. It was not just your standard six-sided die, but that was there and only one of them. There was a four-sided die, which looked like a pyramid. There was one eight-sided, one ten-sided, one twelve-sided, and, of course, one twenty-sided die! Each role corresponded with a number, and that number corresponded with what would happen.

For most of the game, the action part would take place in your imagination. It would all be controlled by a game master or what is called a Dungeon Master. Usually, John was that. He seemed to take pleasure in creating the universe and allowing us to explore. He often exploited and took advantage of some of our immature characteristics and weaknesses, which kind of made it that much more interesting.

"Twenty…ttwweennttyy!" Burt would say as he struck a body-building pose, showing off his muscles as he would occasionally roll a twenty on the twenty-sided die.

This was going to be a guys' trip up to Burt's house. Don't get me wrong, I could've hung out with Cathi. I loved hanging out with Cathi, but I needed to hang out with my friends also. This was not okay with Cathi, but I sold it as a chance for her to hang out with her friends. We had found out that Burt was joining the Navy soon, and we all wanted to hang out one last time before he left. It was something of a "going-away present" to him! We wanted to show him a good time with his friends so he wouldn't forget us. Nothing illegal, no drugs (we *never* did that!) but a lot of cheap alcohol and general stupidity.

Cathi was visually annoyed but ultimately took it all in stride. She took the opportunity to actually go to a party that her ex-fling Joe was attending. I only found out about this because I called Cathi when we arrived at the upstate house, and she managed to tell me that she was going to a party! She knew that I wouldn't like this, but I felt like it was her way of almost teaching me a lesson!

"How dare I hang out with my friends and not include her?"

"How dare I have a life without her?"

We argued on the phone for about half an hour, but there was nothing I could do. She went to that party, and there was nothing

I could do about it. I had, after all, left her to go upstate with my friends.

We hung up the phone after several minutes. I screamed and yelled all sorts of profanities and at the top of my lungs about her to my friends! Words that I have never said to or about a woman before…at least not in front of them!

"WHAT A BITCH!" I screamed. "SHE IS A CUNT!"

That was said out of complete rage, a strong bit of alcohol, and honestly a moment of male ego! "I have never used that word to describe anyone, let along someone I was in love with and was going to ask to marry me in a few months."

"SHE DID THAT SHIT ON PURPOSE! SHE KNEW WHAT SHE WAS DOING!"

I think she made sure that I knew that her ex was there. I believe that she also *had* to make sure that she told me just to make sure that I felt that it was my fault! As I had mentioned before, Cathi and my relationship had grown to be extremely insecure over the years, and I felt that she had to go out of the way to punish me! I really felt that it was done on purpose. So much so that we were only really happy when we were in each other's arms! I knew in my heart that I was going to marry her, and I felt that I was going to propose that summer, but I still wanted to make sure that I did everything that I wanted to do in life before that day.

Basically, we really only fought because we were *both* very insecure and really jealous if the other one had a life without the other. I don't think I was like this at first, but she had a way of building up my insecurities and really messing with them.

The five of us spent the entire trip playing D&D, playing cards, filming silly skits, and drinking cheap beer. As the evening started to wane down, Rob emerged from his room wearing a one-piece, bright-red, flannel pajama with what had what could only be described as a dump hatch on it that had white buttons on the back on each hip that allowed access when unbuttoned to his bare ass… hence the name that we gave it as a "dump hatch." He was pretty proud of getup, but we made fun of him. Not at first, but the bashing eventually caused him to only make that a one-evening item of clothing…and with good reason!

Bob was pretty much the only one I trusted not to sabotage me in my sleep. The other guys I had known for a few months or even years, and I honestly didn't and couldn't trust each of them not to do something evil to me. Just to get into our memory lure forever would not be something I would want! To be laughed at for all eternity was not something I wanted to give ammunition to for a laugh!

So I was paired with Bob, and we shared a room.

The very first morning while we were up there at Burt's house upstate, Carl and Bob went for a walk down the snow-covered path. The rest of us—John, Burt, Mike, Rob, and I—looked out the window and saw the two of them walking about half a mile down the road. Of course, we had to open the front door and spend the next few moments calling each of them by name and hearing our voices echo in the woods. It started out with just a question.

"Booobbb?" I howled out just to draw their attention, my voice echoing in the canyon.

That was followed by me with several inaudible words and phrases, "Did you get lead sag-pipe scrambled eggs and the carburetor?"

That was, of course, followed by silence.

"What?"

"The blue one?" I followed it up with.

Again, silence until he realized what was going on.

"Dick" echoed in the hillsides!

That was amusing for only about ten minutes or so before I started looking around for something else to do. There was not much fun in that after all, but that did bring up some hunger issues! We decided to have lunch eating all the good food, which I'm sure they wanted but they could not object because they were half a mile down the road! By the time they came back, we had cleaned up any remnants of what we had just devoured. They were none too happy, but most of us had a full stomach having devoured a healthy serving of eggs, potato wedges, and toast.

We then went out into the woods that surrounded the property. Armed with various style BB pistols, one made by Coleman, one by Daisey, we all trekked in the woods shooting haphazardly into nothing and everything all at once. Then one of those idiots came up with a very stupid idea.

Okay, it was me.

And I was not really sure what I was thinking about! I wanted to "shoot across John's bow" and make him jump! I cocked the air cylinder back, making sure to only do one pump, I didn't want to hurt him too much!

I missed.

Not thinking and caught up in the moment I guess, I actually reloaded my BB gun, making sure to only pull the air cylinder down once again and shot toward John.

Within seconds, John's back arched, and he screamed out in pain, "SOMEONE SHOT ME!"

The game was suddenly over, and thank goodness that it only lasted a few shots before we all came to our senses! Of course, John, to his credit, only made my life a living hell throughout the rest of the trip by placing little sighs of BBs and various signs of trying to put me in pain to remind me of my idiocy, but other than that, he didn't retaliate too badly.

CHAPTER 5

A Trip Up to Tommy's House

IN LATE SPRING OF 1986, Tommy organized a trip up to his parents'
house in upstate Bloomville, New York. It was a three-hour drive to
the distant village that I had never been to before. It was a time to
do a getaway from the doldrums of everyday living and visit a new
place to explore! Plus, it was the time that Cathi and I could go away
with each other to just relax and have some fun. We had a three-car
convoy with nine people. The first car was Tommy's, a four-door gray
Chrysler Cordoba. In that car was his friend Monica, who actually
was Mike's, our drummer from the band's, girlfriend, and Joe. Joe
was Conrad's and Tommy's mutual friend. Conrad's cousin, Michael,
was sitting in Conrad's car, a tan Chrysler LeBaron, along with Lisa,
Conrad's girlfriend. Cathi and I were in my black Volkswagen GTI,
and we were in the middle of the convoy. We kept in contact with
each other as agreed by each of us to be on channel 27 on the CB.
This way, if anybody got lost or whatever, we were able to keep in
contact with each other.

Tommy's Cordoba was the first in the convoy, followed by my
car, and Conrad's car was last. The road traveled up and down the
mountains and several long stretches of highway as we gradually got
closer to Bloomville. Conrad's car had somehow managed to be the
first car as Tommy's Cordoba slowly drifted back. Before I realize it,
Tommy was not visible in my rearview mirror any longer.

"Tommy?" I said in the CB handset. "Where are you, man? Is everything all right?"

Tommy was quick to answer. "Hey, guys, be careful! A cop just whizzed past me with his headlights flashing! He is chasing somebody!" answered Tommy's panicked voice over the CB radio.

Of course, I immediately took my foot off the gas pedal and quickly looked up to the rearview mirror. Conrad also slowed his car down. There in the rearview mirror, as Tommy had said over the CB, was the cold blinking headlights in the far-off distance of a car gaining fast! I was going 65 mph, so he had me going at least 80! His headlights were blinking high beams to low beams, on and off, on and off, on and off! Yep, he was chasing something or somebody all right!

"SHIT!" I looked over to Cathi.

Faster and faster, the blinking lights came up from behind us!

Conrad was slowing down, also startled by Tommy's warning!

The car was merely a few hundred yards away now, still doing a very high speed with his headlights flashing when Tommy's voice came over the CB radio.

"FOOLED YOU! HAHAHAHA!" Tommy's evil chuckle came over the CB as his Cordoba blew right past us.

A few miles on the road, we pulled into a large two-story building with a covered wooden deck. The driveway was long enough to hold all the cars and emptied out into what appeared to be a small general store. One by one, we got out of the cars and slowly unpacked the vehicles.

A few of us got into Tommy's Cordoba and went to a local mall near the house. We thought we would try to pick up a couple of rafts that we could use on a local lake by the house. We ended up walking into the KB hobby center that was in the mall. There we found a couple of rafts, and also there was a section of stuff that was on clearance. They had several different items that were on clearance for laser tag! It included a helmet, a vest, and rifles! A virtual starter pack!

Of course, we all had to buy one. In fact, we bought the last four that they had left! One for each of us! Conrad, Tommy, Joe, and one for me. Like four junior high school kids, we couldn't wait to go back to the house to play!

The upstairs in Tommy's house, there was a long hallway that led to two bedrooms and the bathroom on the right-hand side. The master bedroom was at the very end of the hallway. There was a stairway on either side of the hallway. One led up just in front of the master bedroom, and the other one came up just in front of the second bedroom. All in all, it was about twenty-five yards from the hallway.

We must have played laser tag for the better part of the first day! It was so much fun! The four of us were just playing in that hallway for the better part of three hours. Since we had only four complete sets, and five of us wanted to play, one of us would have to sit out every so often.

After some time, we then decided to grab our belongings and go food shopping to pick up our supplies for the weekend. Of course, the four of us decided to wear all our wonderful laser tag outfits. Each of us all wore the black vests, the dark gray with black-and-red striped helmets, and a holster that was made to look like leather with the pistol carried in it. We walked into a Great American in Bloomville, New York, in a sort of formation. We had to shop for our supplies for the weekend, and this made it all worthwhile! A bonus was that Great American had their own store brand of merchandise, and all had a Mega label on it. For instance, there were Mega fish sticks, Mega crackers, Mega butter, or whatever. We spent the better part of a complete hour using that joke on every aisle!

"Look, they have the Mega beer that we need!" I said in a deep voice.

We were all dressed in laser-tag outfits. I can only imagine what those people had to put up with that night!

We returned back to Tommy's house where we unpacked and stocked the refrigerator with our newly found Mega bounty. Tommy had brought up a video camera for us to film various creative scenes that we would all sit and act out. They were all without scripts so basically ad-libbed everything, which at first was kind of silly if not just plain stupid. But as the alcohol consumption intensified, the company barriers seemed to come down. Tommy played bartender and had this unique (at least to me!) ability to make what was called a *mudslide* shake.

He put into blender ice cubes, which he crushed, some vodka, a dash of coffee liqueur, and some sort of cream liquor! On top of that, he put a dollop of whipped cream. In my eyes, he was like a mad scientist! All I ever drank was beer. Cheap beer at best! Of course, there was also an endless supply of that, but everyone lined up for the mudslide milkshake drink that I thought that Tommy had created! In reality, it was actually a drink that was popular in many bars, but as I was not a bar person, it was new to me! Therefore, we all got very drunk really quickly or what we used to say "hammered."

For as long as I've known Tommy—as I said before, Tommy always had a pretty good sense of humor—I didn't know he was into filming various stories and comedy improv scenes! Now we would be able to capture the essence of our drunken mayhem for all to see many years now. We would film silly drunken skits, made-up stories that we would make up on the spot, film them, and just sit back and howl at what we had just done.

In one such scene, Conrad, Tommy, and I came up with a spoof on the American Express line "Do you know me."

We went upstairs in the hallway where we were earlier playing laser tag, and we thought it was funny if Tommy came up to a closed door. He glanced at the camera with a smirk and held up the American Express card. The door was locked, but he was able to pick the lock using the card, and it opened the door to Conrad sitting on the toilet.

"Do you know me?" said Tommy in a stern but questioning voice. "Well, you should. I JUST OPENED YOUR DAMN DOOR!"

Conrad sat there for a moment looking shocked! He slowly raised his hand and tapped on the white bathtub that was to be filled to the top with water right in front of him. Submerged and under the water but out of view from the camera's eye, I quickly surfaced and came out from under the water. I was covered with a white towel that covered my body, so I was hidden from the scene.

I surfaced out of the bathtub and screamed "No, do you know me!" and I, too, was also holding an American Express card, once again using the company's catchphrase.

We laughed and were quite proud of ourselves! Once I dried off, we quickly went downstairs to plan another scene and to refill our mugs of the fine mudslides.

The next morning, we had pancakes, bacon, and sausage with toast from all the packages that we picked up at the Great American the night before. Tommy went outside and had an electric pump to blow up a large dark-gray raft that those who wanted to attend would go down the local river together. It was a sort of lazy river, but the river was man-made, and there were several spots where they had built small waterfalls to increase the flow. That didn't mean that we couldn't have splash fights or whatever, but it was just a relaxing tour down the river. The conversation was pretty widespread, focusing on the laser tag and the breakfast we had. We spoke about different things we're going to film that night.

Somewhere along the conversation on the river, Tommy informed me that there was something that he felt necessary to tell everyone. Although he said he had never seen it before, he felt that the house was haunted by a little girl. She only came out a few times while he was there but was looking for her mother.

"Late at night, I kept hearing a low crying voice," Tommy said, and almost immediately, the entire river was all quiet while he spoke.

"'Mommy…is that you?' She would say in an eerie voice."

That was quickly laughed at by who was on the boat, but it was obviously a nervous chuckle and one that we really didn't believe any-way. In fact, I actually forgot about it within seconds; I just nodded my head to keep the conversation going.

After about two hours of just floating and relaxing down the river, we went back to Tommy's house and filmed another evening of some silly stories. There was the interview with Freddie Krueger from *A Nightmare on Elm Street* in which I wore a Freddie Krueger mask. I spoke like Freddie Krueger, which made for a lot of enter-taining dialogue! It was all made funny by the alcohol consumption, and looking back the next morning, we would surely see how foolish this was! Once again, Tommy's mudslide milkshakes began to flow, which seemed to make it that much funnier.

At the end of the evening, we all staggered up to our assigned bedrooms. Conrad and Lisa had what was the designated master bedroom at the top of the stairs, with Cathi and I sharing the middle room in the hallway on the right side. Among other things, spending time together with Cathi was something that I really enjoyed. She was my girlfriend, and after all, I was a guy! Any chance that we can get together and fool around was a bonus!

Taking it slow as I knew we had all night, we spent about ten minutes with what I would consider foreplay and were just starting to truly get excited. The mood was getting rather heavy when all of a sudden there was a clicking sound, almost like a pull string!

"Mommy…is that you?" It was followed by a shrill and eerie crying!

For a second, I was startled but quickly jumped out of bed! I grabbed my pants and sprinted out the door! There, gathered in the hallway, was the entire drunken crew from the trip all laughing at my expense!

CHAPTER 6

Cards

ONE EVENING, CONRAD CALLED US all together to play cards. Jimmy was Conrad's good friend and was becoming a good friend of mine also, but Conrad and Jimmy were pretty much inseparable. They shared the same sense of humor and knew how to make each other laugh. Jimmy had the stereotypical "Italian" look about him. His hair was kept about two inches in length and combed straight back. There was no part in the scalp; it was like he just combed it straight back. He apparently really cared a lot about lifting weights from the first time you looked at him though. He was tone and buff to the point that I could never truly even imagine myself doing that! His friend, Kenny, was also there. Kenny was the same age as all of us, twenty-six, and I was told that he worked with Jimmy as a contractor or a handyman. Their mutual friend, Craig, was also invited. I had met Craig a few times before with Jimmy as he was part of Jimmy's inner circle of friends.

We each cracked open a bottle of Corona beer and sat down to play cards. Conrad had bought a package of Dutch Masters cigars to smoke while we played cards. I had smoked a few cigarettes in my life and never really enjoyed it and certainly never wanted to smoke ever again, but I had always seen people smoking cigars while they played cards. I bought into the advertising and marketing of it. I didn't enjoy it, but it was just for the environment of playing cards. I dragged the smoke into my mouth; I held it in my mouth for a couple of seconds and exhaled it. In my mind, I was smoking. Yes, I had bought into the illusion of how "cool it was to smoke." That lasted all of maybe eight minutes or one cigar when I realized just how disgusting it was though!

Conrad was a regular smoker, so this was nothing new for him. Apparently, he was up to at least a pack a day and sometimes more. A few times, I had actually seen Conrad cough up a dark-brown-colored mucus-filled spit that was really gross, but that was usually after he ran or did something physically active. I still felt it was a disgusting habit and one that I would never get into, but there I was smoking a cigar for the card game that night.

Conrad lived in a downstairs apartment of a ranch house in Seaford, Long Island. We had to go down a flight of stairs in the back of the house to access his apartment. It had one bedroom, a living room, a small kitchen, and a bathroom with a full shower. It was a nice place. The upstairs house was a ranch-style house that I think was owned by an older couple although I never met them. That was just what Conrad said anyway. I think they had one son, but we never saw him.

We lit up the cigars and grabbed a few beers. Jimmy had picked up a couple of six-packs of Sam Adams Lager, and there was the usual supply in Conrad's refrigerator of Coors Light and Budweiser. I brought some chips and popcorn. We started the night like we used to do with a standard game of five-card draw poker.

That is the game that we are dealt five cards facedown, followed by a round of betting on those five cards and you are able to discard three cards to increase the value of your hand. Unless, of course, you have an ace in your hand and then you can get rid of four cards. But usually, that's a dead giveaway to everyone else that you have nothing and you're hoping for some sort of magic to happen. It's a very simple game, but it allows us all to warm up so speak.

Kenny won the first and with a full house—three kings and two sevens. There wasn't much gloating, however, as it was just the first hand, and the pot was very small at this point. Then because Kenny dealt the first hand, I was next at the table to deal, and, therefore, I had my choice of the game selected. I was partial to a game called

"Follow the Queen" in which the anti was $.25 to play. You would be dealt seven cards, circling around the table. As each card was placed in front of each person faceup, you could slowly see how each game would start out. Some players were dealt a hand that they can make something out of. We had a pair or a straight, something worth value to bet on. But if a queen of spades came up, it would end the game immediately, and each player would have to re-anti the original $.25 that we all put in to start the game.

"Suck it up!" I said as I threw the queen of spades to Jimmy.

That was followed by various sounds of happiness and some screams of frustration because they had a good or bad hand. As I was dealing, the Queen of spades came up two more times, and I had to restart the game.

Eventually, Jimmy won that hand, and as it worked out, he was also the next person in line to deal. The game went on for a couple of rounds with us smoking the cigars and cracking open a couple of beers each when there came a sound from the upstairs apartment that took us all by surprise. I had mentioned that the upstairs house was occupied by an elderly and that they had apparently gone away, leaving their twenty-two-year-old son to watch the house. He apparently had a girlfriend, and they took the opportunity to fool around. Normally, that would not make any difference to us, but under these circumstances, a bunch of intoxicated guys playing nickel, dime, quarter poker with nothing better to do, it became a sport! Every time his girlfriend moaned in apparent ecstasy, called out his name, or made any noise once so ever, we made up a rule that we had to each put in a quarter into the pot!

At first, this was sort of funny—$.25 here and there!

Then another!

Still another!

After about three minutes of each of us giggling like children, I raised my voice and said what I thought needed to be said, "This guy better cum soon, it's costing me a fortune!"

As the words were leaving my mouth, Jimmy chimed seconds later, "I got a shit hand anyway!" But he didn't drop, in fact nobody did!

Finally, there seemed to be only silence from upstairs, and we finished up the game.

Conrad won the hand, and it was almost $22 in nickels, dimes, but mostly quarters. He was able to get a few bicentennial quarters which seemed to make him happy because he actually had a collection of those. Of course, now that we all knew that, we would have to go out of our way to get them from him!

Friends are like that!

Conrad was the big loser that night with his bicentennial quarter collection ended up being spread out to each of us but mostly Kenny!

CHAPTER 7

Starting the New Job

WITHIN THE NEXT TWO YEARS, Multiline Technology seemed to not grab hold of the manufacturing environment as everyone had thought. Although the company appeared to be growing fast at first, I think they were caught in a situation where they tried to grow too fast. However, I did learn a very valuable trade at that company: how to negotiate price and guarantee needed delivery to meet production deadlines. Unfortunately, this manufacturing field started to slowly dry up. For several weeks, there was talk of somebody within the purchasing department who would have to be let go. There were only three people in the purchasing department that could have been let go: myself, Manny, or John. I kept wondering every day if this would be my last day! The stress was unbearable. After a while, I actually knew it was going to be me! *Why?* Because I knew they wouldn't let John go as he ran the entire department and he was the boss. He knew everything that had to be done, in the company and where to get it. Manny was a foreigner. And I hated to say this, but he was the only Afro-American in the entire company. They almost *had* to keep him. Even though he was hired after me, which he was, I felt he was safe. So that left me! I finally couldn't take it anymore. One day, downstairs and near the company fax machine, I had my chance to confront Roderick. I walked up to him and asked him directly.

"There is a lot of talk around the office lately…" I said to Roderick. "Am I going to be let go?"

I was laid off from the position at Multiline Technology due to the company having some financial issues. As I had surmised, they had overestimated the market growth within that environment and didn't anticipate the decline in marketing revenue. I found myself looking for a work once again, but this time, I did have something going in my favor. Not only had I built up knowledge of how purchasing works and buying in general, but I had also built up quite a decent number of contacts within the manufacturing world. Word had gotten out to many of the vendors that I used to purchase material for that I had been let go and I sent most of them my résumé. That was one of the good things that had come from that job. I had access to many different vendors that I had been in contact with. I grabbed my Rolodex when I had been asked to leave Multiline Technology and was able to send out twenty or so résumés, looking for work. I felt I had a hand up in getting a job with those companies because at least they may have known me when they saw my résumé if I sent it to them. I must have sent out twenty-five or so résumés to various companies that I had interacted with within the first few days of me being home. After just one month of collecting Social Security, I was called by two companies that I had sent my résumés to. One was a company named Air Powered Tools or APT, which was a company that built different high-quality air pistons and various other items for machinery. The second was a company called Sager Electronics. Sager Electronics dealt with electronic interconnect, power and electro mechanical, or IPE (industrial production equipment) components. With both companies, I knew less than nothing about the material they sold, but like everything else in life, there had to be a learning curve. APT offered a low base salary but was strictly a commission position. It was therefore something I wasn't too comfortable with. I contacted Sager, and after only one interview, they hired me. I was hired as one of the sales reps for inside the warehouse.

The office was about a forty-minute drive each way from my house to the facility in an industrial park in the town called Hauppauge, Long Island. On my first day, I was put in the back room, which was actually more of a stock room. There were four aisles of gray steel shelving that were forty inches in width, eighteen inches deep, and seventy-two inches high that ran the entire length of the stock room. That ran more than one thousand yards deep. Each shelf formed a small cubby where the merchandise, delivered by us at the company, was moved and placed inside large blue totes that were taken off the truck. The items were placed on the shelf that corresponded to a number and could be "picked" for an order. I was apparently going to be a middleman for the company, not responsible for ordering but for just doing the manual labor of shelving the merchandise. I wish I had known this prior, but as the old proverb says, "Beggars can't be choosy." This was not what I wanted to do. There was something to be said about buying or purchasing. I liked doing that, but I was not into anything like inside sales. I spent several days wondering what I was to be doing. I would never get on the phone and talk to customers about what was needed. I don't know what I was hired to do exactly. I wasn't doing anything in terms of buying or selling! I was just pulling stock and running around with the inventory. I would sweep the stock room and basically just be a qualified stock person! This was not what I wanted. I didn't really like what I was doing, but what choice did I have? Basically, a semi-trained monkey could be taught to do the same thing. However, it was a job.

Carmine was a little Italian man that ran that back room. He was a tiny man with thick gray hair. He had a beer gut and looked like he smoked a large assortment of Cuban cigars, but he didn't smoke at work. Joe was the only person that I usually spoke with. Joe was a little overweight, and he also was the stereotypical Italian with the white undershirt and wore his hair combed straight back and not parted in the middle. He was funny and made me laugh often. Joe knew the job well as I think he had been there for a few years already. "Once a week, someone brought in bagels, which was kind of a nice touch." There was a sort of roll call, so the same person wouldn't have to buy the bagels all the time. I was to be next Wednesday, and since I was the apparent new guy, I wanted to make sure that I got what everyone liked! Most days I had to race in on Bagel Day because my favorite of cinnamon/raisin was also a few others' favorite, and I didn't want to be stuck with something that I didn't want! Garlic or onion would be a reason to not grab the free food! I wasn't so keen on egg bagels either, but free food was always good!

Those large plastic blue bins that I spoke about before were now placed in rows of four bins tall and five deep off the truck. They were placed in rows of two or three deep. They had to be emptied, and each item had to be checked in and compared to an inventory sheet to make sure we received it and it wasn't counted wrong. Then we had to put the items in the assigned shelve and inventory location for a buyer to send out for others to use. Again, not rocket science. This was not something I could be seeing myself doing every day for the rest of my life! I had to remember that this was a stepping stone to build up my résumé. I was at Sega for about two months, but the position was not really what I wanted. I mean, I was told that it was a purchasing position, but I felt that I was more of a glorified stock person, emptying these large blue totes that were filled with merchandise ordered by other people that were brought into the warehouse and loaded by the shipping dock. I had to unpack those totes and place the items on the corresponding labeled shelves in the stock room to be picked up by various sales reps as needed to be shipped to various contractors. I then had to do just general housekeeping in the stock room that included sweeping and organizing the workspace. I had done this in Caldor, and while it was not below me by any means, I just couldn't see myself doing this my entire life. I found that within a short amount of time, I truly did not like the position. However, I had no choice but to stay within this company until I found another job. I am a believer in the statement that you only look for a job when you have a job but don't need a job. You will have the best bargaining power of any new position, and you will only take a job that you want. I really don't think that I had given this job a chance, but I felt that the position had no future in it for me.

CHAPTER 8

Instigator Man!

MORE THAN A YEAR AND a half had gone by when Tommy announced another trip to his parents' house in upstate Bloomville, New York. Over and over again, we decided to develop some characters based on the conversations we had. We decided to film several new scenes based on our conversations.

Tommy made still another mudslide that he had made for us a few years back that had us all intoxicated rather quickly, and the party started again! After several other video scenes of what we thought was hilariously performed in a fine alcohol-induced frenzy, we agreed to do a scene that was developed ad-lib and was based on Cathi and my continual disagreements and arguments. Tommy took pride in the fact that he would say little things to make Cathi and I disagree and sit back and watch the fireworks. That was becoming more and more obvious to everyone involved, and Tommy created a character called Instigator Man. This was simply because it almost became a joke that whatever he said caused an argument for a discussion between Cathi and me!

Tommy wore a black cutoff sweatshirt with a large white letter "I" for Instigator Man across the front of the shirt. That was a name that Tommy gave himself as he took pride in trying to get Cathi and me into silly disagreements. Instigator Man was a character that he created for himself. Basically, he just would say things that Cathi and I would argue over. It was just a word sometimes, but that would often start the discussion and arguing. Hence, the name: Instigator Man.

Tommy always wore a full black beard as long as I had known him. In this scene, Tommy wore a white bandanna on his forehead. He often wore a bandanna when he played on stage also, so this was nothing new. Conrad wore a bright-red shirt, and it was covered with a blue cape that hung neatly around his neck. His beard was a lot lighter than Tommy's, almost an orange, but he too, wore some sort of a silver headpiece which kind of resembled what Wonder Woman, starring Linda Carter, wore in the show from the late 1970s.

The scene opened up with Tommy standing with his hands on his hips and Conrad looking sternly with one eyebrow higher than the other. Both have a proud grimace on their faces.

I was the announcer, with an off-camera voice speaking in an authority-like manner. "These are not ordinary men…they are men from another world…another time…another dimension. But here on earth? They are heroes. No, not the cold cut kind but the real American kind! And although they have lived their lives being ridiculed by others with names such as wimp, jerk, and mama's boy, they stand for truth, justice, and the American way. They are Instigator Man and his sidekick, Tattletale Boy! Superheroes for hire!"

The scene opened up with the two heroes sitting at a table drinking. Suddenly, a knock came from the door off camera!

"Shit! There's someone at the door!" a surprised Tommy spoke in a panicked tone.

Both men quickly started clearing off the table from various bottles of alcohol. Within seconds, both men sat down.

"Come in," beckoned Tommy.

Amy, one of Tommy's cousins with long curly brown hair that was long enough to cover her face, came staggered into the scene. Obviously inebriated, she struggled to compose herself.

"I need your help…" she slurred, her long dirty blond hair hiding her face and never allowing her to look up from the table or at the camera.

Tommy pushed back her chair. "Sit down, fine lady in distress, damsel lady. What seems to be the problem?" he said with only a slight pause.

But Amy, looking hard to the left, was unable to hide her laughter as well as Tommy was, causing him to say, "Easy. Take deep breaths. Not too many, I would get excited!"

"Breathe slow…" followed by Conrad in his high-pitched woman's feminine voice.

"Fema-Man took my husband away!" Amy said in a slurred, drunken-like lisp.

Tommy punched the table. "Fema-Man is back! Don't worry, fine young lady, damsel in distress! You go home and wait for our phone call! We will take care of it. Me and Tattletale Boy!"

They both looked at each other and let out an evil yet very silly "Hhhhhuuuuuheeeeeeeeeeeeee."

Amy had disappeared suddenly from the scene, and all that remained was a close-up of Instigator Man and Tattletale Boy.

"Fema-Man is back!" Tommy spoke as he pounded his fist on the table. "To the Bat Cave!" he said, looking down toward Conrad. Conrad looked up and pulled on Instigator Man's shirt.

"What?" asked Tommy, almost annoyed.

"We don't have a bat cave," Conrad said in his high-pitched feminine voice, shaking his head in sorrow.

Instigator Man was obviously taken aback. Staring directly into the camera and again punching his hand he hollered, "WHY DON'T WE HAVE A BATCAVE?"

Shaking his head and taking a deep breath sigh of disappointment, he returned his hands to his hips, leaned back, and spoke in a loud voice once again, "Then to the Bat-mobile!"

Conrad didn't move but simply looked up to Tommy, shaking his head no.

"It is only a flight up, let's run!" said an exasperated Tommy.

The two crime fighters turned briskly and appeared to start to run out the room, but Tattletale Boy's cape appeared to get tangled underneath his feet, and they both tripped down to the floor with the thud.

The scene switched to me wearing a pink low-cut sweater, a matching pearl necklace, and a pink bow my hair. I had one huge hoop of an earring in my left ear and what appeared to be a hickey on the right side of my neck below my ear. My head was down, and my ear was to the floor, listening as the two heroes agreed and started to run up the stairs.

Fema-Man spoke in a sarcastic tone, "Oh no! My archenemies are running up a flight of stairs to fight me!" Fema-Man spoke in a strong, feminine lisp. "What will I do?"

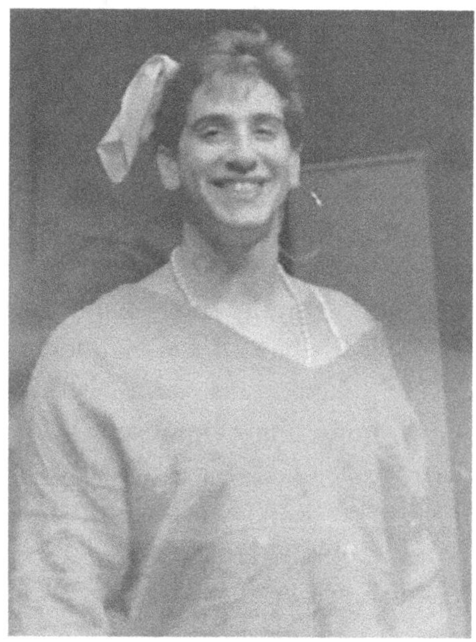

A very drunk Fema-Man

Behind me and playing the parts of Fema-Man's evil henchmen were my girlfriend, Cathi, and Conrad's girlfriend, Lisa. Both were wearing pretty much the same outfits; a gray sweatshirt top and jeans with a colorful lay around their necks.

I pondered "Hmmm" and placed my hand on my chin while I was pacing back and forth. I then circled around with the henchmen who were doing the exact same steps, like they were choreographed. Step by step, each one was exactly at the same moment. Finally, at one point, I looked over my shoulder to the left and saw the henchmen doing the exact same thing, so I threw my hands in the air, like John Travolta in *Saturday Night Fever*, just to see if they would follow my moves! To my shock and honestly to my overall joy, they did!

"You're on your own!" Fema-Man screamed, his hands flailing about.

Suddenly, music from Kool & the Gang "Boogie Nights" started to blast, playing a dance melody disco sound.

Fema-Man danced up to the camera lens with his own arms flailing, saying, "I love a party!"

Dancing back and surrounded by his two lovely henchmen, they all danced happily to the beat of "Boogie Nights." Gradually, the camera's eye rose to view the light fixture as it slowly faded.

The scene switched to Tattletale Boy laying on top of Instigator Man.

"Please forgive me! I didn't mean to trip you!" said Tattletale Boy in his high-pitched voice.

"I'm sorry… I'm sorry…"

"All right, all right! Just get off of me! I can't breathe," replied Instigator Man. "Just get upstairs and get Fema-Man!"

Tattletale Boy got up quickly and ran off camera as did Instigator Man, but as Tommy rose, he realized that a lone clothespin was fastened to his briefs by his balls.

"Aaggh!" he screamed out in pain. "Damn, kids! You can't count on them for shit!"

The scene switched over to upstairs where Fema-Man and his two henchmen were still dancing to the Kool & the Gang song that was piped in from the speakers.

"Boogie Nights…"

"May I cut in?" asked Tattletale Boy in his feminine voice.

In a shocked voice, Fema-Man said, "It's Tattletale Boy! That wimpy little sidekick of…of the dude…"

A voice, obviously Tommy's, came from the side off camera and almost in a whisper said, "Instigator man…"

"That's it, Thank you, Instigator Man!"

Turning to the henchmen, Fema-Man continued, "Girls, Disperse!"

In ran Instigator Man who appeared to be gasping after for air from running up the flight of steps. His hands were on his waist as he struggled to catch his breath.

"Good work, Tattletale Boy!" called out Instigator Man!

"Thanks" was heard in rebuttal.

Everyone's circled with their fists up ready to fight, but we circled around each other without throwing any punches. Fema-Man suddenly put in his hands and apparently surrendered!

"I give up!" Fema-Man said. "I give up."

"I knew you would give up," said an overconfident Instigator Man! "Because we are Instigator Man…"

"And Tattletale Boy!" chimed in Conrad.

Fema-Man, with his back to the heroes with his hands up, then punched both of the heroes directly in the balls!

Both the heroes were left gasping for air.

"Silly, silly, silly!"

Fema-Man quickly turned and danced off toward the camera with his arms raised above the shoulders in apparent victory.

"Girls, prepare the traps!" He ran to the camera flapping his arms to the henchmen.

The scene switched to Instigator Man and Tattletale Boy sitting being tied up to various chairs with their backs together.

"You've escaped my clutches once too many times," Fema-Man said in his soft, overconfident feminine voice.

"As you can see, gentlemen, I have shackled you both hands and feet to the stairs, and now I will forcibly let you listen to the anthology of the Beach Boys!"

Fema-Man turned, let out a simple "Ha-ha" laugh while he danced away. Instigator Man just screams out "No!"

"Why are we not wearing on *bat-cups*?" Fema-Man asked no one in particular.

"I didn't think so…" He shook his head as a classic Beach Boy intro song played.

Instigator Man, in obvious pain, was unaware as Tattletale Boy was suddenly able to free himself and ran off camera to turn off the music. He returned and quickly untied Instigator Man!

"Tattletale Boy? How did you do it?" asked Instigator Man. "How did you handle listening to that stuff?"

"I was wearing my anti-Beach Boy…" He paused, apparently trying to find the right word, but then is joined by Instigator Man. "Earmuffs!" In his ears, he had to wear rather large, unseen white tissues that were in his ears.

Both heroes obviously were relieved and slowly walked to the camera to which Instigator Man put up his hands and shrugged.

"Why didn't I know about this?"

The scene then switched to Fema-Man bragging to his henchmen who were sitting cross-legged just behind him.

"Ladies! I succeeded! I killed them and…"

Suddenly, he let out a surprised gasp!.

In walked Instigator Man and Tattletale Boy.

Shocked, Fema-Man quickly turned to the two henchmen. "Ladies, Get Them!"

Tattletale Boy was the first one that approached Fema-Man and threw a punch that had little effect on Fema-Man. Fema-Man then kicked Tattletale Boy in the chest, and as he fell backward, he held up a one-by-one-foot handwritten sign that said "Ouchhhh!" as he fell backward.

Instigator Man followed immediately to which Fema-Man said "Oh, another one!" and kicked him also in the chest, causing him to fall backward.

This time, Instigator Man held up another handwritten sign "&%@#$!" as he was falling past the camera.

Fema-Man turned to the two henchmen. "Hey, this gives me an idea!"

They performed a kick line with Fema-Man humming a song, "Dada…dada…dada," ending with everyone smiling and placing their hands in the air above their heads.

In raced Instigator Man!

"Still again!" screamed Fema-Man. Instigator Man was quick to answer though!

"You will never get away with this, *never*!" He leaned toward Fema-Man with his hands on his hips.

Fema-Man then pushed his hand into Instigator Man's chest, shoving him backward.

Instigator Man looked down and was almost shocked as Fema-Man's hand pushed the huge letter "I" on his chest, and he shouted, "You poked me in my 'I!'" He then turned to Tattletale Boy and said, "Get him, boy!"

Tattletale Boy moved toward Fema-Man and tried to kick him in the chest. Fema-Man caught the heel and tossed Tattletale Boy back into Instigator Man, but as he did, he held up a sign that said "BAM!" that we all stopped for a moment and pointed to.

Fema-Man took Tattletale Boy's leg and pushed him to the ground who then held up a sign as he fell past the camera and hit the ground, "OUCH!"

There was a moment of a chase, and Instigator Man came to a sudden stop!

"Screeeeeeeccchhhh."

Instigator Man said to the camera, "Pretty cool, huh? Not so fast…"

"Give me a break already!" said Fema-Man, thrusting out his arms.

"Break? We'll take him!" He called out, turning to Tattletale Boy, "Show him!"

Tattletale Boy reached into his pocket and grabbed an Instamatic picture which he held up in front of Fema-Man's face! He very quickly realized that the picture was upside down and quickly turned the picture around.

"The duke!" Fema-Man said aloud as he brought his hands up to his mouth!

"You better well believe it!" Instigator Man said in a deep, superhero-like voice!

"I would follow him anywhere!" said Fema-Man, almost fluttering toward the photo of John Wayne.

Fema-Man followed Tattletale Boy around the room following the picture.

"This way, boy, we'll take him right to the prison!" said Instigator Man.

Fema-Man high-stepped right behind Tattletale Boy who was holding the photo high right in front of his eyes walking backward.

In the next scene, both heroes stood with their arms crossed next to each other.

"Once again, we beat evil." Stood a stoic Instigator Man.

"And it wasn't with the luck," added Tattletale Boy in the high feminine voice.

"Because good is good…" said Instigator Man.

"And evil sucks," they both said in unison.

From off the screen, a good voice called out, "Okay, fellas, that's a wrap!"

Tommy broke character first, walking past the camera but saying in a high-pitched feminine voice, "Thank God, I have to go to the bathrooooom!"

That was followed by a very low, raspy Brooklyn dockworker-like voice of Conrad who tried to light up a cigarette, "I fuckin' quit…"

The director called out, "Good job, everyone. Good job!"

The scene closed with Conrad clicking on his lighter that didn't light and screaming in a low Brooklyn dockworker accent, "I need a *light*!" as he stormed out of the scene.

We were all pretty proud of each other with what we felt was a pure comic gold trip.

Satisfied with the several fine comedy sketches that we had done that night and with much of the alcohol consumed and finished by us all, one by one, we all agreed to call the night. It was at this moment that Conrad actually took me aside and asked me the following question.

"Hey, do want to switch girls for a few hours?"

I laughed at first, thinking it was a joke.

"Can you imagine?" I said to Conrad.

Then Conrad followed it up though and made it all too real. "Lisa will be asleep in a few minutes, and you could just go in there and fool around awhile with her, and I will go in with Cathi."

He was serious!

Reality made you sober up really quickly.

I quickly sobered up and thought that this was probably more than the alcohol talking. This was not a good thing. Not only would it be wrong morally to do this but it would be considered *rape*!

Rape is not funny!

I shook my head, called it a night, and went upstairs. Cathi was waiting for me upstairs in the bedroom, and I crawled into bed with Cathi that night. I tried to forget what was just said and just play it off as a drunken comment.

CHAPTER 9

The Following Days

WE RETURNED TO WHAT I thought was our mundane life and continued band practices the following week. Nothing was said regarding Conrad's late-night proposal to switch girlfriends for the evening, and I just figured that it was a drunken moment, one that I should forget about, for that was what it had to be. That made absolute sense to me. It was a moment that I would try to forget and *never tell anyone*! I mean who would believe me anyway? Surely, it was just a drunken moment that I'm sure Conrad probably didn't even remember! How could a friend, *my friend*, a person that I had honestly felt was becoming my best friend, truly say and mean that question? It had to be the alcohol talking! I would just pretend like it never happened and go on with my life.

That was until Conrad took me to the side once again a few days later after band practice.

"You know when I asked you the other night if you wanted to switch with me, I was serious, right?" he told me.

Shocked, my mouth dropped open! I think I just sort of smiled, shook my head, and walked away from the idiot! I *never* thought that something like this could ever happen! I mean, maybe in a pornographic movie, but not in reality! Not to me! How could I even look him in the face ever again? How can I be friends with him? This was a guy that I thought was becoming my best friend? An evening of alcohol and silliness was one thing, but now we had time to mull it over and present a sober, well-thought-of attempt! I wanted to run… to basically hide! Certainly, I could never say anything about this to anyone. Certainly not Cathi! I mean she would never believe me anyway! Then again, who would? They would say that I was just imagining things or that Conrad would never say or do anything like that! I "must've just mistaken or misunderstood him." However, I was *not* just imagining it! *This had happened, and he was serious!*

A few days later, I walked into Cathi's house, and she was on the phone with him! Apparently, he called her a little while before I got there and was having a conversation with her like there was nothing wrong with that!

"Oh, he's here now…" she said to him over the phone, "would you like to talk to him?"

Apparently, he didn't, and they hung up the phone within seconds.

When I asked Cathi why he would call and not talk to me, what she said was he wanted to see what we were doing tonight. She honestly had no idea what he was doing and thought it was just him being a friend who wanted to hang out. I, on the other hand, saw it for what it was!

That fucking dick was setting the stage for himself! Trying to drive a wedge between Cathi and *me*! Apparently, I was the one who was overexaggerating everything in this relationship and was seeing things that just weren't there because of *my* jealousy!

Bullshit!

He was innocent and wanted nothing from her but to be friends? I was the one who was wrong?

What a *fucking asshole*! *How dare him*! What a crock of *shit*! *My friend*! Surely, everyone would say I was just imagining this, but I was the one who saw that was really happening! Who would believe me?

Unbeknownst to me, sometime before Christmas, Lisa had actually broken up with Conrad. She had her own reasons I guess, but she broke up with him. I'm sure Conrad was heartbroken as we often had spoken that he and Lisa would be together forever. He didn't say a word to any of us! I had no idea this happened!

Conrad must have been crushed! As I was finding out, Conrad had a pretty large ego! I mean, let's face it, he had what I feel was a great voice, was what I would guess was good-looking, and people thought he had it all! Lisa was an extremely attractive girl with a great personality, and quite honestly was I felt completely out of my reach, not that I would have ever thought she would be with me! All this only added to Conrad's image! That's why when he asked me "to switch" with him months ago, it was kind of only a fantasy for me! Not that I would have ever done that, but I think many people, me included, saw the two of them as the perfect couple! He was in fact only after one thing, and when that was gone, he had to prove himself.

Apparently, Cathi was now in his sights.

Over the next few weeks, I walked into the house, and Conrad managed to be on the phone with her again and again. Each time saying that he was looking to see if we were hanging out, and then each time I wanted to grab the phone, he would find a way to end the conversation and just hang up. Never speaking to me! I would question Cathi, and each time, she said the same thing!

"He wants to know what we were doing tonight," she would tell me.

That *fucking* idiot *never* told us that Lisa had actually dumped him, but he was still letting us believe the image that they are were still together and nothing was wrong!

The last time I asked Cathi just how long they were on the phone, she replied, "I don't know…a half an hour or so?"

"Are you serious? What did you talk about?" I asked, raising my voice.

Don't you see what he's doing? I shouldn't be jealous? I shouldn't be insecure? Here was a guy that I thought was becoming my best friend, and he was doing this to me? He was overstepping the boundaries and was becoming a *real threat* to not only me but my relationship with Cathi! She really had no idea he was playing for her!

That was when I told her what was going on and what he had said to me. This was what I felt was his true intentions and *she made me feel as if I was wrong*!

Her reaction?

"You are imagining things! He is innocent, and you were just being jealous!" she screamed at me. "He's with Lisa!"

We argued unmercifully for several hours each time that happened. Each time getting more and more heated. She kept saying that I was just being a jealous person and that she and Conrad were just friends! I had nothing to worry about!

I believed her. She honestly believed that, *but* I knew of his true intentions.

Then on Christmas Eve, after walking on her on the phone with him on the phone with him for the fourth time, I *finally snapped*!

I stormed out.

I didn't need this *shit* any longer. If she didn't put an end to it, I *would*.

CHAPTER 10

Forced to Start Over

I spent that Christmas in 1990 alone and just knowing that the situation with Conrad had ended things with Cathi. No matter what I said or was able to show Cathi as proof that that "fucking dick" was doing to "us," I was wrong in her eyes, and I just couldn't do this anymore. I was hurt and honestly couldn't do this anymore! How I let that dick put a wedge between Cathi and me was *disgusting*! I honestly felt that I just shouldn't have to compete for her love because she didn't believe me and thought that I *was wrong*! I should have called out Conrad and told him to just *back the fuck off*! I knew what he was doing and to *get the fuck out of my life*! I was *so* tired of this entire situation, and I just couldn't handle it anymore!

To walk out on Christmas Eve and leave this situation forever was what I felt was the only option for me. I was really hurt that she was going to let this asshole break us up, and I was upset with the fact that I couldn't do anything to stop it. I spent Christmas the next day hanging out with my mom, my sister, my aunt, and my cousins in Brentwood, Long Island. We had gone out to eat every major holiday to the Radisson Hotel on Motor Parkway in Hauppauge. Every once in a while during dinner, my mind would go back to the situation with Cathi and Conrad and what drove me to where I was at that very moment in my life. I felt sorry for myself, but I knew I was right. I was after all going to ask her to be my wife! I wanted to spend the rest of my life with her! Why I didn't confront Conrad was beyond me. I think I was now suddenly tired of trying to prove my love for Cathi. Conrad had shown me this about my relationship: true love can't be and shouldn't be *this* hard!

The following day, feeling a bit restless to say the least, I decided to give that girl, Colleen, from work a call at home and asked her how her holiday was. Colleen, in the few weeks prior to my breakup with Cathi, I had told her just about everything that was happening with Cathi and me just in conversation. I felt that it would be really great to hang out with her just to talk to someone who was not in this immediate circle. I was attracted to her when we first met at Multiline months ago, but because of my love for Cathi, I had backed off, but now? Why should I?

She was surprised to hear from me at home, but I had gotten her home number a few weeks prior because of something that was happening at Multiline Technology. The company had given out an emergency call list to every employee to use "just in case" the need arose to contact someone if needed. Why would someone have to contact someone in this company in emergencies beyond me? Once upon a time, I had organized a get-together for something business related. Never realizing that I would use the list for personal gain, I rummage through the list and found her number. I dragged up the courage to call her, and I placed the receiver to my ear as the phone rang.

After a few seconds of opening pleasantries, I told her my story and said that it would be really nice to talk with someone who was more or less neutral about my situation. I wanted to see if I was overacting and just losing my mind. We spoke for about half an hour before I asked her if she wanted to hang out and get lunch. As we were just friends within the company walls, I felt that I had convinced her that I just needed someone to talk to. That was all I wanted at that moment. I honestly wanted nothing more than to just talk.

She agreed to do go out for lunch, and I would pick her up. She told me how to get to her apartment, a complex in Farmingdale. It was a Fairfield Courtyard North in Farmingdale, and she lived with her parents on the third floor. I parked in front of the building and walked to the front double doors and into the vestibule. It was a four-by-four little glass room that opened to another set of locked glass doors. To the left, there was a wall of little white buttons all in a gold frame with a corresponding name and apartment numbers of the person that lived in that apartment right below it in typed letters. Associated with each bell were tiny boxes that were associated with each apartment for I guess their mail. Nervously, I searched for the little white push button of apartment number 331 and pressed it, ringing the doorbell for her apartment. Within seconds, a woman's voice crackled through the three-by-three speaker that was just above the doorbell I had just pressed.

"Hello, who is it?" came the voice.

I knew right away that I had got the correct apartment.

"Hello, is Colleen there?" I said into the voice box even surer of myself now. "It is Peter Licari."

"Oh, hello. I'll be down in a second," came Colleen's voice.

Within moments, Colleen came stepping down the stairs to the front vestibule and opened the front door. She had a little longer than shoulder-length dirty blond hair, and she was wearing blue jeans and a heavy black ski jacket lined with a bright-yellow stripe. I nervously gave her a kiss-on-the-cheek hello, and we strolled out to my car.

We drove to the Farmingdale Diner near her parents' apartment complex in the town of Farmingdale, New York. I had never been to this diner before, but I think that every diner is pretty much the same. I ordered a muffin and a glass of juice. All she asked for was a cup of tea.

We must have spent an hour or so in that diner, just talking. I had spoken to her at work, but this felt different. I felt that there wasn't any piece of the conversation that I felt that I was competing for her attention. I wasn't worried about the clock and how much time we had before we would have to get back to work so that I wouldn't piss off my boss at Multiline. It was just Colleen and me, and for the first time that I knew her, I felt comfortable enough to just talk with her.

The conversation went on for what seemed like only a few minutes, but actually, we were there for a few hours. It felt so easy to speak with her! She didn't offer an opinion unless I ask for it, and she just listened. We started just speaking about many things: current events, people at work, etc. It was so nice not to be aware of stuff that she would get offended by or cause a fight with. We spoke about everything and nothing at all! We agreed to go into New York City by train in the morning. Again, it was to just hang out with no commitment and no expectations. We were just friends, and that was all. It was very pleasant, and that was the way I wanted it! We were just friends, getting to know each other. I was never a city person, but I felt like doing something different with her.

We walked and did some of the touristy stuff that New York offered. I felt alive and carefree. At the end of the day, we got off the train at the Farmingdale train station. Her apartment was just across the street from the station, and I had parked right in from of her building. I stalled a bit as we walked up to my car, and she turned quickly and gave me a quick kiss on the lips. We agreed that I would call her later, and that was it! I wanted to hang out with her again, and I hope that we would soon. It was only when I got home that the burden of Cathi and what Conrad did hit me hard again.

That New Year's Eve, Colleen and I went to a local bar by her house to watch the ball drop. I picked Colleen promptly up at one o'clock on Monday, December 31, 1990, at her parents' Fairfield Courtyard North Apartment complex in Farmingdale. I figured that I would take her out to a nice dinner at some restaurant before we would head over to the Changing Times Pub on Melville Road in Farmingdale. I had never been there, but it was close to Colleen's apartment complex and was right across the street from Farmingdale College, so it should have been a hopping place. Regardless, I just wanted to be with Colleen.

The mood was festive with every television tuned to the exact same channel. Each on a forty-inch television that was hanging just above the mahogany-stained oak bar top was blaring the same channel. *Dick Clark's Rocking New Year's Eve* party was playing on every 40-inch television set in the bar firmly on channel 7, WABC New York. Dick Clark was wearing a black sky jacket with about a 4-inch white circle patch sporting the black letters of the station call letters, ABC.

"We have got just about three minutes before the big ball drops, and everybody here attention will be drawn to that 6-foot in diameter 250-pound sphere lowered by cable, 208 balls on it that are all red, white, and blue when everybody's eyes down there are glued to that…" spoke an exited Dick Clark.

"Eleven fifty-seven and one-half minutes, Happy New Year time will be upon us here on ABC!"

The picture then focused on the ball hanging from the top of Times Square.

"Red, white, and blue in honor of all forces all over the world, particularly those in the Persian Gulf who are watching New Year's Rocking Eve this year, our hearts and minds are with you, folks. This is the eighty-third year of the ball drop in celebration here in Times Square!"

It had been a bad few months, and right at this moment, I was only thinking about how much I really wanted to kiss Colleen.

"With one and a half minutes, keep your eye in the ball, it will descend that 77-foot flagpole…there is an army of eight men and women up there who will lower it by hand…hand over hand…it's a cotton-bound steel cable. When it hits the bottom, you'll hear a roar from the crowd in one minute from now…"

The crowd and the atmosphere were growing to a fever pitch. I was looking at Colleen, and she was looking at me.

"Thirty seconds, and it will be 1991. The eighty-third Annual Ball Drop Celebration Live from Times Square in New York. Twenty seconds. Before the roar goes up, let us wish you all the Happiest of New Year's, 1991 arrives in ten seconds…eight…seven…six…five…four…three…two…one… Happy New Year!"

I leaned into Colleen and shared our very first open-mouth kiss that seemed to last forever. At least in my mind! I never wanted it to end. Slowly though, we loosened our grip on one another and parted into each other's hands. We stayed at that bar for another few minutes, and then we agreed to get out of there. She was amazing, and that kiss was even more than I had expected! We turned and slowly figured that we would head out to the door.

One woman in particular blocked my way and staggered toward me. She apparently intended to give everyone at the bar a kiss as a Happy New Year gift! Never one to want to kiss total strangers, I immediately decided that I needed to get past this drunkard! She seemed to have had taken part in just too much of the holiday cheer already and was making the rounds to wish everyone a Happy New Year.

"Haaaappppy Neeeew Yeeeeaar." She leaned into me for a kiss.

There was *no way* that I wanted this to happen! I ducked and managed to get past those groping lips with just an open-air hug. The smell of alcohol was clearly emanating all around her.

Colleen and I managed to hightail it out the front door without further issue. I grabbed Colleen's hand and led her out to my car. Unlocking the door, I let her slide into the front seat of my car as I walked around to the driver's side. The Changing Times Pub was just a few miles from her folk's apartment, and we were there within a few minutes. We spent about fifteen minutes outside in front of the building, just making out before I thought that we probably should just call it a night. I mean I didn't want to, but I thought that maybe we couldn't go any further, at least not here and at that very moment. It was in fact a *great evening* and one that I didn't want to end, but I assured her that we would have many more in the future! I got out of the car and walked her to the front vestibule. We kissed good night again. I told her that I would call in the morning and watched as she went inside the apartment complex.

CHAPTER 11

Spring Fest 1991

WE GOT TOGETHER WITH THE Nassau Center in Woodbury, New York, to see if there was something that we could help out with at one of their charity events called Spring Fest. The Nassau Center is a Center for Developmental Disabilities and is committed to helping children and adults with different abilities achieve their dreams by overcoming barriers to living, working, learning, and enjoying recreational opportunities in the community of their choice. This was a festival that they rented a stage that was in the parking lot of the school.

I had asked my friend, Joe, to play with us. Joe had a very earthy sound to his voice and once again fit in with us. He had a tough job replacing that idiot Conrad, but he had a really good voice. Conrad had a strong voice that allowed us to play Journey, but Joe had more of a soul sounding that many people could sing along with. It was good and to the point! Richie was on lead guitar, and there was nobody better in my eyes for what we were doing. As I have said, he was just a full musician. Tommy was on rhythm guitar and had great harmony and some lead vocals, and John was the drummer. He kept very consistent time on drums. Nothing overpowering, but he was *very* consistent and played with the best!

We opened up with "Slow Down" by the Beatles. We had one big speaker right in front that carried all the vocals and a low mix of the music to the front. All of us had our own amps, but this one was placed in the center to balance the sound out. At first, just one girl ran up and stood directly in front of the big speaker, like a moth to a light. She was wearing a white shirt with pink shorts, and she was also wearing a bright yellow visor to keep the sun out of her eyes. It hid her vision for the most part, so we didn't see her eyes! Then we went into "The Night Before," once again by the Beatles. She was joined by a young man with these blue gym shorts that I would have worn in the gym class when I was in elementary school! He was standing doing an Elvis, circling his hand around his body. We went right into Elvis Costello's "Pump It Up," which seemed to bring everyone out dancing! A great rendition of Oingo Boingo's "Fool's Paradise," which I think we nailed although I don't think anyone ever heard of it in this crowd, but it made us happy!

The "dance floor," which was the parking lot floor, was slowly starting to fill up with people all dancing to the sounds, swinging their arms, and stepping to the rhythm. After a few seconds, I grabbed the microphone for a version of Chuck Berry's "Roll Over Beethoven," which I had really heard done as the Electric Light Orchestra's version, so that was the way I sang it.

I heard from the crowd a little girl call hollered, "Play a slow one!"

That was all Richie needed to hear.

"A slow one? I don't think we play any slow ones."

Then he went into a song in a 1-4-5 progression *very* slowly.

"Yeah, we don't play anything like that. The next band plays nothing but slow songs." It was followed by some laughs from the crowd. "Am I right?"

"Oh, I don't know!" screamed a voice from the crowd.

"I'm telling you," Richie said into the mike, "half their songs are slow, right?"

He continued, "You'll like this one…listen to the lyrics."

Then he started thumping into the groove of "Crawling from the Wreckage" by Dave Edmonds. We went right in "Good Girls Don't" by the Knack.

"Thank you very much!" said Richie into the mike. "I like the people in the front, they're clapping…the people in the back… I don't know…"

We went right into "Louie, Louie" by the Kingsmen. The crowd was in a frenzy, dancing all around when we went into "Twist and Shout" by the Beatles followed by "I Saw Her Standing There," also by the Beatles. A call came out from a few people in the crowd that Cablevision News Channel 12 was here filming.

There were a few kids in the front of the stage shouting out, "One more!"

We went into "Good Lovin'" by the Young Rascals to much applause. That was always a favorite of ours.

Then Richie stepped up to the microphone. "This is the last one for us, but stick around…" He continued, "There is a great band coming up after us. I wanna thank you all for showing up. It is a beautiful crowd…a beautiful day. I love you all, and I don't even know half of you!"

CHAPTER 12

Spring Fest 1992

WE HAD A GREAT TIME playing the Spring Fest in 1991 that we decided to see if we could play it the following year, 1992! This year was a bit different in the members that we were able to get. Joe, who sang great as the lead singer for us last year, was unavailable as was John the drummer! If we were going to play Spring Fest this year, we would have to get several replacements. Luckily, we had a large assortment of people that we could tap to play! Richie, Tommy, and I were a strong nucleus musically on vocals and harmony, but we didn't have a lot of time to learn everything and choose what we were going to sing. We ended up tapping my friend, Paul, who was on my softball team, Black Sox, which played a modified fast-pitch softball.

Paul was Sal's cousin, and Sal was a good friend of mine that I had worked with at Caldor. He was a great guy, and we had actually shared a *lot* of things personality wise. Not for anything, years ago, he actually had dated Cathi, but that wasn't how we had met. We met at Caldor, and we shared a lot of mutual friends. That was how we formed my modified fast-pitch softball team, the Black Sox. We were all friends at Caldor.

Anyway, Paul was comfortable in front of an audience and knew a lot of the songs that we wanted to play. A *huge* plus was that he owned all the equipment and had a place for us to practice! We would be *nuts* if we didn't take this opportunity! Anyone who wanted to play *and* had all the equipment would certainly be welcome. We found that we could cover the person if he was not that good, but again, he had all the equipment! We were under a tremendous rush to put this all together anyway. We needed a drummer, and we got one literally a week before the gig! Pauli would be the drummer; he was in the inner circle with Tommy, so he was used to all the songs that Tommy played and was pretty good…at the very least he kept decent time. Plus, I wouldn't have to remember another name!

We opened up with "Frustrated" by the Knack and went right into 'Wild, Wild West" by the Escape Club. The sound was pretty good with Paul's speakers and the public address system, but there wasn't a big crowd dancing like there was last time we played here. I was wearing my Black Sox softball jersey, number 17, which was my lucky number, and I wore it in honor of my father's birthday. Under that shirt which hung open, I wore over a hot pink shirt with the name of the Nassau Center for Developmental Disabilities all with light blue jeans. Richie was wearing a white-collar shirt and black jeans. Tommy was in blue jeans and a black tank top, and Paul was wearing a tight black tank top.

A young black girl with an orange balloon danced in front, rocking to the beat of the music. She was dressed all in white—white shirt, white high socks that stretched all the way over her legs, and a white "Gilligan" cap. At my first glance toward her, I saw that she had one leg thinner than the other, but it was skinny compared to the rest of her body. She just rocked back and forth to the beat with the thin leg anchored to the ground.

We went right into Elvis Costello's "Pump It Up." A pale young boy was punching the air and moving all around in front of the stage. He was wearing pink gym shorts that were a little too short for him and a light royal-blue shirt. We then went right into a song by the Romantics called "You Got Me Where You Want Me."

"You got me where you want me…" Richie was singing lead.

I stepped up to the mike. "Now would be the time to dance! Do we need a formal introduction?"

Richie started the opening chords of "What I Like About You" by the Romantics, which we played really well! We played that for about two or three minutes, and then we went right into "ROCK in the USA" by John Cougar Mellencamp. We played that for another two minutes until we went right back into "What I Like About You" by the Romantics.

I stepped up to the mike again. "Hi, honey!" I said into the mike as I waved to Colleen. I had asked her to come to the event, and she did! She had never seen me or my band play, so I was very excited to see her there. "We got a couple of the dance floor," I continued, "but I think we need a little more."

"Yeah, yeah!" someone screamed from the crowd.

Then I stepped in front of the microphone again. "It could get no hotter than this," I said. "Really, people, before we get into any more of this, the guys you see before you…they're going to hate me for doing this. Two weeks ago, we hated each other. We still do. Two weeks ago, we weren't together for a full year, and they donated a lot of time. And I personally want to thank them. Tommy, guitar. Richie, lead guitar. The lead singer, the drummer, we never even played together for a full year. He donated all the equipment. The lead singer, Paul. The drummer, I don't even know his name, Pauli. Thank you." I continued on, "That was from the heart, guys, it really was…"

Then we went right into "Twist and Shout" by the Beatles. That girl who was dressed in those white shorts, white shirt, and was wearing the white baseball cap holding the orange balloon was still dancing right in the front. We started playing "Mony Mony" made famous by Billy Idol and sang at weddings all over.

Paul jumped down off the stage with a yellow supermarket bag filled with stuff.

"Come on over here, everybody, get some Lays!" he said, and I remember looking at Tommy.

"Did he just say that?" I mouthed to Tommy.

"Come on, get some Lays!"

Then Paul said in the spot that everyone usually says some dirty things, "HEY, LET'S ROCK AND ROLL!" screamed Paul but not once but *three times*!

"HEY, LET'S ROCK AND ROLL! HEY, LET'S ROCK AND ROLL!"

We started playing "I Hate Myself for Loving You" by Joan Jett. Right in front was my sister, Nancy, who was dancing to every song!

"Okay, we need a little audience participation now!" said Paul.

Then we right into "Shout" by Otis Day and the Knights, highlighted by me screaming "Yeah, yeah, yeah!"

"Now we are going to go a little strange," I said. "Like we aren't already!"

We then started "Crawling from the Wreckage" by the Dave Edmund Band, but in this case, Richie had the perfect voice for it.

I started to yodel. "Yodel…"

"I learned that from him!" I pointed to Richie. "Yodel lay hee hoo! Yodel lay hee hoo! Yodel, yodel lay hee hoo, hoo, hoo!"

We went into "Good Girls Don't" by the Knack. I sang that, and it went over well, but at the beginning, Tommy's microphone didn't work, and Paul had to replace it. Paul was very quick to change it.

"We are having a lot of technical difficulties," I said it the mike. "We knew that song a long time ago…we really did!"

Richie was quick to chime in, "SHUT UP, PETE! We never knew that song! He doesn't realize that there is a lot of other things going on, not just us!"

We then played "I Wanna Be Sedated" by the Ramones, which had a bass solo at the end of the song, which Paul announced to the crowd to a spattering of applause.

Tommy started "Summer of '69" by Bryan Addams to much fanfare. In front, there were no fewer than three people all doing the exact same dance: rocking back and forth on one foot then the other back and forth in unison. The girl with the balloon, now a yellow one, and dressed all in white with the white "Gilligan" hat was rocking just like everyone else.

Then we went into "Hang On Sloopy" by the McCoys. Paul sang lead on that one also.

"Hang on Sloopy. Sloopy, hang on!" Without missing a beat, we went right into "Louie Louie" by the Kingsmen.

We ended the song to a splattering of applause.

More yodeling came from me.

"Thank you. We are going to do a sound check right now… joking! It's just a joke," I said.

Richie jumped in with a sarcastic "Ha-ha!"

"This is the last song!" I said. "There is a great DJ and a great band following us!"

"Right this very second although after this last song, there is a sing-along," I said. "In the atrium and those who want to *sing along* can go in the atrium after this song, or you stay out here and party with the DJ…"

Richie chimed in, "Or you can stay and help us move all this crap off stage!"

We went right into "On the Dark Side" by John Cafferty and the Beaver Brown Band, and we ended the day right there.

CHAPTER 13

Penn State

COLLEEN WAS ACCEPTED TO PENN State University as an economics major, and she was going there after this summer of 1991. We had grown together a lot since we first started dating exclusively that New Year's Eve. How would I handle the separation with her going to Penn State? I called her every evening, but speaking on the phone was nothing like seeing her! Before she left, we hung out just about every day, but now she was far away, and I couldn't handle being alone.

After dating for about nine months before Colleen went to school, I decided that I would visit Colleen at Penn State University one weekend in October. I would pack my car, leave early and visit my girlfriend on the weekend of October 3, 1992. She managed to get us tickets for the Penn State college football game in which the Nittany Lions, Penn State's team, was playing Rutgers Scarlet Knights from Piscataway, New Jersey. I had never been to a real college football game, and Penn State football was as big as it could get!

I settled down in my Black 1983 Volkswagen Rabbit GTI with dark maroon red interior with yellow hair-thin stripes. I had applied a Batman sticker stick on the back left just above the left taillight and on the hatch.

It was going to be a five-hour ride, but I was excited! Not only was I leaving Long Island and going to see my girlfriend, but I was seeing a place that I had never seen before! I was really excited to see a college football game also! I had never even thought about that. I was not really into college football as there wasn't a good college football team in the news on Long Island. I just had to get across the Cross Bronx parkway and the Throngs Neck Bridge! I had a brand-new radar detector that I had bought for the trip, and I was set. I had no idea how it worked, but I guess all I would have to do was turn it on! It worked like a charm as it hummed a few times, and I was able to slow down until I passed the speed trap. I think I was able to avoid three tickets!

Colleen gave me precise directions to get to her housing on campus. She was in what was called the Pollock housing area. That area was the second-largest residential complex, with nine traditional coed residential halls. The majority of the halls were reserved exclusively for first-year students, which Colleen was. I followed her hand-written instructions to a T, and we finally met up with each other! It was actually rather easy to find her!

God, it was good to see her.

She took me into her dorm, and I was immediately overtaken by the powerful scent of the Subway sandwich shop that was in the building. Everything carried the scent of freshly baked bread that was pleasing but actually began to get rather nauseating by the end of the first day! I could only imagine if I had to stay in that building for a long time.

We stayed for maybe half an hour before Colleen actually said to me that we had to get ready for the game. She had tickets for the Penn State Nittany Lions versus New Jersey Rutgers at Beaver

Stadium. There wasn't a second level, so the seats could have been far back, but they weren't! Our seats were on the field level in the left-hand corner of the stadium on the thirty online or so, but we were about forty rows back from the field. Who cares though? I was at the game and was having the time of my life with my girl! I asked Colleen to paint a blue paw on my cheek which was the symbol of Penn State. I wanted the entire experience!

Penn State won the game over Rutgers, 38 to 24, and I had a great time!

After the game, Colleen showed me around the campus. We walked around and went to as many of the sights as we could. There was actually a fair that was going on, on the campus also, and there were rides and games! Colleen won a small stuffed animal, a duck, at one of the games. We lined up with four or five other people to shoot water guns in a clown's mouth. As the water from the water gun stream hit the clown's mouth, a balloon would expand until it popped! She beat me and everyone else to win the prize! A little duck which she gave to me!

What a beautiful campus!

After spending a great weekend exploring the entire campus with Colleen, I drove home. After seeing so much green and beautiful landscape at Penn State, I made a mental note as I was driving home just how gray with cement everything got when I came over this one hill by the Throngs Neck Bridge on the way home. New York for me was depressing in that way.

Everywhere I looked, everything was dark and dirty cement. Most with cracks haphazardly through the surface, and others had moss or something growing throughout. I tell you this might be why some people hate New York City!

CHAPTER 14

I Have to Make a Choice

THINGS WERE GOING FINE WITH Colleen and me in the winter of 1992. Colleen had actually slept over at my apartment in early November, and we had honestly started to plan for when she was coming home in the spring. I actually was falling in love with Colleen, and I hope she felt the same for me! I couldn't wait for her to come home each time she left. I was falling big for her, and I started telling people in my inner circle that I think I had found the one for me!

I was sitting at home, watching *Bugs Bunny* when the phone rang in my bedroom. I had my own phone number from the house phone so I could have sort of have my own independence! I needed it for my job hunt anyway. My mother didn't want an answering machine, and I felt having my mother answer the phone would not create the perfect image for companies anyway. Plus with my mother, I really couldn't guarantee that I would get the messages anyway!

"Hello," I said as I picked up the phone.

"It took me a long time to actually pick up the phone to call you," said the voice.

I thought about it for a moment, but I had no idea who this was.

"Who is this?" I asked.

"Who would have guessed that I spend four years with someone, and you don't even recognize my voice? It's Cathi," said the voice.

Wow, Cathi was calling me? I was now totally confused. I forgot where I was, and WHEN it was, but slowly, everything came back.

We were on the phone for maybe ten minutes. It was like we had never missed a beat! We had been apart for nine months or so, and it was like no time went by at all! We were just talking about basically nothing really, as if everything that had happened had not and we had never broken up. But it was really good to hear her voice. I told her that I would call her later on that night.

I spent the day thinking of Cathi. So much so that I even called Colleen Cathi!

That was bad.

I hadn't even missed her *until* that moment! It had been almost nine months? Had it been that long? How long had it been? My mind was mush. So much had happened since we last spoke. What was going on with her? I wanted to see her! I didn't know what to do anymore.

The least of all was with Colleen. I called her at her school and told her that I was confused and I had to be honest with her. She was understanding and basically told me that she didn't want this anymore and couldn't do this. She broke up with me that night. I understood that, but I didn't know what to do. I loved Colleen, I really did, but I also loved Cathi.

Now what was I going to do?

I fell back on my comedy! That was the way I handled *everything* in my life.

So I thought it was a good idea to make her laugh in only the best way that I knew how! I decided to take the stuffed chicken that she had won for me at Penn State and show various ways of me about to torture the stuffed animal! I was wearing a paper bag to hide my identity, but she would know it was me! I would mail here the photos up at school for her to, I would hope, enjoy! Obviously, it was just a joke, but it made me feel good, and I thought that it was funny…*really funny*! Of course, I didn't mean anything by it, but I just wanted her to laugh!

SALLY
FIELD
FLYING
NUN

Later that day, I called Cathi again and asked her if she wanted to hang out again.

CHAPTER 15

Still Another Job

So I continue to send out résumés in hope of finding a new job. Within four months of trying to grow within Sega, I received a message on my answering machine at home asking if I wanted to come in for an interview. I had sent out one of my resumes to LILCO, the sole supplier of electricity on Long Island, and it had reached the personnel department where they had several positions opening! I felt that LILCO was one of the premier jobs on Long Island and one that I would really be interested in! If I got a job here, I would be set for life! Everyone needed electricity, and there was only one place to get it on Long Island—LILCO!

The message was from Mrs. Claire Robinson of the Long Island Lighting Company personnel department in Hicksville, Long Island. The reason that it was considered to be a premium job by many was that there was no real competition within the electric field; everybody needed electricity, and it was from what I hear a very high-paying job! It was what I considered one of the only shows in town.

I wanted to get this job.

I returned Mrs. Robinson's phone call as soon as I could and told her I was interested in coming in for an interview. The interview was at eleven o'clock on Tuesday morning which was the very next day. I told her I would be there and was very excited to tell her about my qualifications and how I would be able to help the company.

Now I had to come up with a way that I could leave the Sega job in the early morning the next day for this interview.

The first thing I thought about was all too easy once I thought of the idea. Rather than telling the truth in asking for a half day because of personal reasons, I came up with the following: I got my cousin, Carol, to call up Sega and tell them that there was an emergency. I had to leave right away as my mother had gotten into a car accident, and she was being taken to the hospital. Carol was one of my favorite cousins and was actually studying to be an actress at the time, so this would not really be a stretch for her. I am not proud of this lie, and in fact, I don't even know why it had to be done at all, but it worked like a charm, and I was able to run out of the building to attend my interview thirty minutes down the road.

The elevator doors opened out into the fourth floor of the building, and I faced double glass doors. I was dressed in a dark olive-green suit with a blue striped tie, and my black shoes were polished nicely.

Man, I looked good!

There, a young woman with short blond curly hair sat behind a huge brown desk. The desk was lowered and hidden behind a shelf like a cubby so that she had to look up to everyone. Behind her, there were several dozen mail slots and a large digital clock that looked like it was made from polished nickel chrome. That hung just below a large painting that said LILCO in strong black letters that was highlighted by a rainbow. To the left of her was an open doorway that seemed to lead into some sort of a copy room. She was sitting behind a huge desk that almost looked like a judge that took up the entire front of where she was partially hidden behind the top of the desk shelf and unless she looked over her. Just in front of the desk were several chrome chairs with maroon cushions. They were several chairs facing the desk which appeared to be where visitors could sit and wait for whomever they had a meeting with in the purchasing department.

Nervous but feeling pretty confident, I approached the woman behind the desk.

"Hello, good afternoon," I said. "My name is Peter Licari, and I'm here for an interview?"

She quickly looked up with a smile and said, "Oh, Ming is expecting you. Just sit down, and he will be up here right away."

She quickly glanced down to her hands and spoke into the mouthpiece that she had wrapped around the head and spoke to Ming. "Peter Licari is here to see you."

A few minutes later, Ming came out from behind the wall. Walking down the hall was a thin Oriental man with stringy, slightly graying black hair and thick round glasses. He wore a dark-blue baggy suit and a light-blue shirt broken up by a darker, almost black striped tie. Partially hidden by the jacket but clearly seen and in the left-hand corner of his shirt pocket was what I recognized as a LILCO company badge. We exchanged basic greetings, and he led me to a small door that was just past and to the left of the front desk. We opened the door, and I was quickly introduced to Mrs. Claire Robinson who was there for the interview also. She was seated behind a table and rose to greet me. She was a relatively tall, thin young woman with straight blond hair which she wore parted in the middle, and she wore an emerald-green dress. I felt that she was a bit younger than I thought she would be when she left the message on my answering machine, but then again, I didn't know what to expect.

"Good afternoon, Mr. Licari, I'm Claire Robinson," she said.

I smiled and shook her hand. We spoke about all the things that the company had to offer and what was expected from its employees.

"As you know, the Long Island Lighting Company is the sole supplier of electricity on Long Island. We are currently looking for a buyer for purchasing agent to purchase various items or contracts that we would need," she started. "You would work with various engineers and contractors as well as our legal team to negotiate and purchase materials and services in the contract side of the house. If needed, you would also purchase for the best price and deliver various materials needed for the entire company."

We spoke about what would be required from me and in the position. I was told that the company had some major changes and was always in the news rather negatively for having the highest electric rates in the country. The department was going out of its way to lower the costs of operating and still maintain the highest standards of surviving in this atmosphere.

"Because we're under the watchful eye of the Long Island media and the political firestorm that is created, we have a lot of procedures that the manager has very strictly implemented," he said.

After a few more minutes, I was told that they were going to make a decision in the next couple of days, and if it all worked out well, I will hear from them by Friday if I was selected.

I didn't go back to Sega that afternoon, thinking that I probably should take the day off at that point. I mean my mother was supposedly in the hospital after a car accident after all! Rather I just stayed home, looked through the paper at the want ads again, and watched TV.

The next day, I went back to Sega and basically continued to lie but said that everything was okay, and I appreciated them letting me go early. I was still walking above the clouds as my mind was at the chance of me having a new position. The day moved slowly, but I was in a good mood. In fact, it moved rather slowly until that Friday when I received a phone call left on my answering machine at home. The second message I had on machine, after a message from my mom, I recognize immediately was from Claire Robinson at LILCO, and she said she had some good news for me. She wanted me to call back as soon as I could to discuss a possible position within the company. They wanted to offer me a position in the purchasing department and wanted me to start by the end of the month if I was interested.

I gave a two-week notice at Sega that following Monday but was told one week was adequate, and as quickly as that, I left Sega. I had just one suit that I wore to Multiline and SEGA, relying on various slacks, several assorted Dockers, and an assortment of colorful ties, so I definitely had to go shopping for some basic suits and business attire. I ended up buying four suits, a bunch of shirts, a few more ties, a new pair of black shoes, and one pair of brown shoes. I did have various business clothes, but I needed to make an impression and sort of growing up with my attire. I mean my work clothes for

Caldor, Multiline, and Sega I felt were less than professional. They were acceptable, but I needed to "show that I was an adult." I was now over $500 in, but that's what credit cards were for, and with my new position, I wanted to show I belong! Plus, I now felt that I had an adult salary, and I should show it.

So on Monday, April 16, 1990, I walked into the Long Island Lighting Company on the fourth floor of the 445 Broadhollow Road with my brand-new dark blue suit, a white-collar dress shirt with a red tie that was striped with black-and-yellow stripes. I walked up to the front desk where I had met a different secretary that day when I came in for my interview, and once again I said my greetings.

"Hi, I'm Peter Licari, and I'm here to see Ming again. It is my first day."

"Good morning, Mr. Licari!" she said. "My name is Roberta, and welcome aboard!" She stood and thrust out her hand as a welcome.

"Ming is expecting you and will be up shortly and should show you around."

And just as she said that, Ming appeared around the corner with an outstretched hand. This time, he was dressed in a dark gray suit but still maintained a blue tie. I followed him around, and he introduced me to several people of various titles. Eventually, I was let into the cubicle and given a binder. I was told that that was the department procedures and the department manager, Anthony, was a stickler for the procedures. I was told that he would back anything up that I did if I just follow the procedures.

The binder was about three inches thick and was filled with things I was unaware of in every aspect. Various rules and regulations were laid out on how to purchase things from materials to working services to how to write contracts according to procedures and rules. I had no idea what all this was about, and I felt that I was completely over my head! Terms like "procurements" and "purchase orders," which I was familiar with from my time at Multiline Technology, but there were others that were very new to me, like "blanket POs" or several more agreements that had to deal with the legal department I was not aware of.

I sat there for pretty much the better part of the day reading everything that had to be done. I was never one to sit back and read with a true understanding though. I've always been a person who learns by doing.

Repetitive use of this knowledge in a working environment would have been the best for me.

I felt very overwhelmed.

Right next to the cubicle that I was in and just around the corridor, I was introduced to Anne and Alan. Anne was a petite young pretty Italian girl and Alan was a slender Oriental or Hawaiian guy. Both were about my age but seemed to have their own little clique. I immediately thought at the time that they were relatively new to LILCO also, and I was correct as they had only been with the company for only a couple of months. They were sitting at the furthest point of the department so they were by themselves, but they offered their help to me in any way that they could. Everyone that I had met had said the exact same thing to me, so I knew it was a friendly office. I did my best and showed my personality to them both, and I didn't feel all that comfortable. I have to admit I kind of felt foolish around them like they were making fun of me, but maybe I was just being sensitive. They didn't know me, and I was trying way too hard to be accepted…maybe too hard. But I just shrugged my shoulders and went on with my day.

I was introduced to Bill who was a senior buyer and apparently would be a sort of mentor to me. I would learn everything that I had to learn in this purchasing department from Bill. Bill had a Barney Rubble from the Flintstones look about him. He had a chiseled face and was slightly balding with a blondish/graying haircut in an almost Dutch-boy-paint haircut. He was relatively portly but not overly overweight, just not in shape. Within seconds, he made me feel very comfortable with his pleasant sense of humor. Also in the cubicle was David.

David was a relatively skinny Oriental man who wore huge oval black glasses, kind of like the kind that Ming wore, but these were almost round, pretty thick, and jet-black. Unlike Ming who spoke with a sort of Oriental accent which you would hear on most TV shows, David's voice had a slow breathy low tone and was somewhat deliberate, like he was contemplating every word that he said. Within a week of sitting with Bill and Dave, I found that most of Dave's conversations ended with one singular phrase.

"It's crazy," spoken in the breathy low tone, and that usually meant the conversation was over.

The purchasing department was split into two separate departments so to speak. One side of the department, or "house" as it was known, bought materials or any material that was needed to complete a job, and the other side of the "house" was for contracts, such as services that a location would need such as maintenance, building structures, snowplowing, or any physical labor that may be needed. Bill, David, and I were now a small piece of the contract side of the house. There were a great many other buyers or purchasing agents handling all the physical items for the company. Items such as springs or wires, bolts, tools, or basic material and needs for the job to get it done. Even some clothing that many of the crew that represented LILCO needed.

I liked handling materials better. You can see the material, but contracts and services, you couldn't really see unless there was a problem. Maintenance of the location or perhaps some snow removal of that location was considered a contract or service for example. There had to be ten buyers alone just handling contracts, and now I was to be one of them. Usually, a senior buyer would handle contracts simply because there were substantial law items involved. I had a lot to learn before I did that, and it really wasn't my area of buying at this point. On the other side of the department and literally around the corner and down the hall were several rows of buyers and purchasing agents handling material. Everything from cleaning supplies, to any sort of "widgets," to various writing implements such as pens or pencils, to even paper or wire for circuits had to be purchased. Everything that had to be used and had to be purchased was negotiated for the best price! That was something I probably would have to do in the future.

Outside of our cubicle which the three of us sat was a hallway where Larry and Jen sat with their backs with each other. They shared a common center island between their workstations. They were the department expediters for the entire department, and they were assigned to take care of any and all deliveries of the various items to make sure that they were on time. For instance, if a purchase order was negotiated with the buyer and had various dates for delivery, those two made sure it all took place as what was written in the purchase order. The only time that these two would see the fine yellow copy paper that was typed signifying a purchase order sort of would be if there was a problem. Usually, the individual buyer responsible for that purchase order would be the one to contact the vendor if it was a problem for the procurement of the item, but sometimes, they were too busy. So the expediters, in this case Larry and Jen, would contact the vendors.

The company had four power stations. Bill, along with a few other buyers, was responsible for the procurement of most of the jobs that the contracts were hired within the various power stations. There were power stations in Northport, Far Rockaway, Port Jefferson, and Island Park. Everything that was needed to be constructed, Bill and a handful of other buyers would receive a requisition for work that was needed from an engineer or what was called a "project manager" as a work order. They would then oversee the purchase of the items needed for that job. We in the purchasing department were responsible to get the items at the best price and the best delivery.

I had a lot to learn.

CHAPTER 16

Streak

IN 1974, AFTER THE DEATH of my father due to Hodgkin's disease, my mother had taken my sister, my brother, and me to Disney World for a week. Obviously, we had been through a great deal with the loss of our father, so my mother thought it was a good idea to go to Disney to help us sort of heal. When we returned, my mother thought it was also a good idea to get a dog.

We had Streak, named simply because she had a white streak on her nose, for nineteen years! She was part Lab/mutt mix. We had other dogs, but we had to buy them for my sister because she always wanted her own dog. Streak became my brother Frank's dog. Oh, sure, my mother fed her and walked her, *but* my brother played with her! That was until he went away to school, then she was more the family dog. My mom would feed her and walk her.

Slowly though, it actually became more of a dislike/hate relationship for my mother. Streak lived until she was nineteen years old and really had no control over her bowels or bladder toward the end. About once a month, my mother would wash the entire kitchen floor by hand, pulling out the refrigerator so she could clean behind it, and when she was all done…that was the moment that Streak would pee all over the floor in the kitchen! Of course, a nice stream had to go under the refrigerator! Streak actually did that several times a week to the point that I thought my mother was going to have a heart attack over this! I had to come home from school or my job as a department manager at Caldor to my mother screaming about Streak, and this was happening *more* than a few times a week! Something had to be done!

I finally had to agree with my mom that Streak could not do this anymore! It came down to my mother or Streak! It wasn't fair to my mother, and I would take Streak to the vet to have her put down. This was the humane thing to do for *both* of them! I couldn't have my mother go through this anymore! I made the appointment with Doctor Decker in Islip, who was the vet that we have had all along, for that Monday. I told my mother that I would come home from work that Monday and take Streak to Doctor Decker to have her put down. Nineteen years was a great run for a dog, and now I had to do the humane thing for my mother and for Streak.

I left work Monday at lunchtime that day, and I went straight to pick up Streak from my house. She was asleep, as was expected, barely stirred as I walked and turned off the alarm. I connected her to the leash and walked her outside one last time. She peed again, and I opened the car door. She climbed in, and we left to go to Doctor Decker's office which was a mere seven minutes away on Sunrise Highway in Islip. He greeted me in the office and asked me if I wanted to go in with her to hold her when the shot was administered.

I didn't think I couldn't do that. Streak meant so much to me growing up. I was already tearing up! I couldn't do it!

I shook my head no. I kissed her goodbye, gave her a big hug, and handed her to Doctor Decker. I turned my back toward her now. I was crying unmercifully as I closed the car door and sat there in my car! I hadn't cried for years, and now I just couldn't stop…

* * * * *

The drive back to the 445 building in Melville took barely ten minutes, and I managed to get a parking spot right in front and to the left of the back entrance to the building. There were only eight spots right in front of the building, and one of them was a handicapped spot. I was usually parked in one of those spots in the morning because I used to get there early as Anthony liked to see as many people as possible in purchasing. Most people in purchasing would try to get there early to show that we were eager or "go-getters," and Anthony liked to see that we were "go-getters." There was no overtime here, as we all were just straight salary, but it still looked good to everyone in the company and for Anthony.

From what I understood, the purchasing department for the Long Island Lighting Company had not been run very well in years past. Anthony was hired simply to clean up the purchasing mess. A few months before I was hired, purchasing had a very bad rap. He already had built quite the reputation throughout the company as a no-nonsense person that you didn't want to get on the wrong side with. He was a well-built, small-in-stature Italian man who had the reputation of a Napoleon-like ruler and ruled purchasing with an iron fist. He was very good for the company and did exactly what he was hired for. I was a weak person by nature, so I was very intimidated by him. He was hired to clean up purchasing, and he did just that.

However, I was always a jokester. I remember one time going to a bar after work for happy hour with everyone from purchasing and walking up to Anthony and asking him if he wanted a drink. He nodded his head yes, and my response was, "You got money?" The expression on his face was priceless, as he slowly reached for his wallet and one that I will not soon forget as I quickly said, "I'm joking! What do you want?"

I thought I got along with him!

I had to get upstairs for the weekly staff meeting. This was the time that all the managers and buyers would meet in the closed-door conference room and talk about their purchasing issue with Anthony. He wanted to be in the loop, and in that respect, he was very good. He was very hands-on on everything and every issue he was aware of. It was kind of funny actually. He sat at the very head of four long tables, each eight feet long by four feet wide and placed together end to end. They were dark walnut, and everyone, all the buyers and purchasing agents from the purchasing department, would sit down either side of the full-length banquet table to be consumed by his power. Obviously, Anthony was seated at the very head of the table, and everyone would tell him what was going on or what needed to be addressed.

I'm told that it was horrible the first time each person would get reamed by Anthony until they knew the key words and what to avoid words that would provoke his vengeance. This was my second meeting since I was a buyer, so I thought I knew what to expect! As I was working with Bill, he would be able to deflect many of the issues for me and *sort of protect me*, but he was not there today.

A question came up concerning a purchase order that I had let actually expire, and now as a company, we were unprotected and losing money.

"What happened here?" Anthony asked me directly.

"Well, Anthony...," I said. "I don't really know..."

Wrong answer.

"What does that mean?"

"I made a mistake, and I take direct responsibly for this."

"Okay...now what exactly does that mean?"

I was lost! Panic set in!

"Um, I made a mistake, and I take direct responsibility!"

"That's great, but what does *that* mean?"

I didn't know what he wanted to hear! "LISTEN, I JUST PUT MY DOG OF NINETEEN YEARS TO SLEEP!" I wanted to scream out! I did everything not to burst out into tears!

"What does that mean? You say stuff like that, but what does it mean? Can anyone else help him to make sure this doesn't happen again?" he finished up with that thought.

CHAPTER 17

Purchasing or Social Butterfly

I HAVE TO ADMIT I wasn't really as committed to purchasing as I was to the social aspects of the department. I thrived on being the social butterfly for many of the issues. I started a lotto pool for any jackpots that would allow us all to dream big. I sent out emails asking everyone who wants to take part in a lotto pool to give me a dollar to be part of it! Downstairs on the basement floor of the 440 office building, there was a stationery store that had a lotto machine. I would collect a dollar from anyone who wanted to play and take it downstairs to play "Quick Pick" lotto numbers. I would then take the numbers that were printed on the official little three-by-four-inch sheets of paper and make photocopies of all the tickets. I would staple the sheets into a little package together and pass them out to everyone that played. I wanted to be the social butterfly of the department!

Of course, we all had a dream that if we would win the big, we just leave, but isn't that what lotto is all about? I then organized a softball team, at first bouncing ideas among other purchasing agents and finally sending out a department-wide email to inform everyone that this would happen. Each member had connections with other departments in the company, and we would set up in various games after work. Of course, Anthony was very intrigued as it showed that purchasing was a family community. It was an arch-pitch softball league, and Anthony would be the pitcher, or I guess he had to be. I figured that we all wanted to play softball and that we would play other departments within the company. Anthony as the department manager really enjoyed that. It showed that we were becoming not only the purchasing department to the entire company but we were becoming friends!

I organized a bake sale for different events, such as the Heart Walk. I asked everyone in purchasing to bake something, and we commandeered the main break room to sell all the baked goods for the charity. I decided to bake blueberry muffins and sell them for the Heart Walk! Apparently, I forgot to include an ingredient so the muffins didn't rise!

Hockey Puck Anyone?

Twelve flat hockey pucks! They tasted fine, but they were so flat, and I quickly became the butt of the joke! Rather than getting a dollar each for the muffins (I had after all baked twelve!), we ended up selling them for four for a dollar!

I did get mocked a lot for that one, but three dollars for the Heart Walk was better than nothing!

I bought myself a brand-new car, Chevy S-10 Blazer! I used my purchasing skills and really pulled off a very good deal! I did my research on exactly what the car would cost, and I figured out exactly what I wanted and how much I was willing to spend. That's what I'm sure many people would do. However, I took it a step further. I went to the same car dealer and spoke to the exact same person for several weeks and told him what I wanted to how much I wanted to spend.

A few times a week, as I was on my way to the gym, I would stop by just show my face and just ask him if there was any difference in the price. He would just say no, and then I would just leave. He had my offer, and I was done negotiating with him. He knew what it would take and what I wanted if you wanted to deal. I figured that eventually he would take my deal if he had a bad month or whatever. I was in no rush to buy a car as I had one in perfect working order. It was up to him if and when he said yes! I was in no rush, and I made that very clear to him.

This went on for several weeks until finally he met my offer! I kind of knew that. When he needed his numbers to go up, he would cave and give me what I wanted. And it was an example of purchasing at the finest! I'm sure that I wasn't desperate, and I waited until he was!

Finally, I got my price!

I opened the door and climbed in. I put the seat in a position where I can best work the gas pedal and was most comfortable for me. I adjusted the mirrors and pulled out of the lot, driving my shiny, almost brand-new 1991 four-door Chevy Blazer that I had wanted. I say almost because it was factory certified, and it was brand-new to me! As I put the SUV in drive, I slowly inched up to Montauk Highway. Wendy's fast-food restaurant was right across the street, and it was a four-lane street, two lanes going in each direction. As I pulled up to the curb, for a quick second, I panicked when the car didn't stop as quickly as I thought it would! I felt my stomach drop in panic as I slammed on the brakes coming to a stop at the end of the driveway!

I did not anticipate that!

Once I got moving again, it took me several attempts to know the feel of the brakes and stop the vehicle with relative ease. Obviously, I was used to my past cars that were much smaller responding to my pressing the break and getting a response much quicker. Within a few miles, however, I was able to adjust.

Breaks are very important to say the least!

I turned down my dead-end street in North Babylon and pulled up to my house. My mother and sister came out from the garage to see what I bought. It was at that moment that I thought about getting my car in the garage. I never anticipated that it would have any issues with this, but I suddenly panicked when my mother asked me about bringing the car into the garage!

"It's gonna fit, right?" asked my mother.

I never thought of that. It was a standard-size, two-car garage! How could it not? Surely, this would fit! It will be a little snug, but there was only one way to find out.

* * * * *

During department meetings with everyone sitting around the table listening to my boss demanding explanations for what they had done to warrant their paychecks on certain purchasing events and why they had done what they had done for the company, I found myself drawing people instead of paying attention. At the end of those meetings that I had zoned out and drew a fellow purchasing agent, I would show anyone that wanted to see the person that I was sketching! Eventually, I got quite the reputation for drawing people! Anything for a laugh!

So it's no wonder that I was passed over for various promotions, and my salary reflected that! If I was just graded on how I influenced the atmosphere and the overall environment that worked in the department rather than dollars and cents, I probably would've done very well financially.

However, that was not reality, and it wasn't for me. I was so trapped to stand out in my little world to grab the attention that I wasn't a very good purchasing agent.

CHAPTER 18

Budgeting and Cost Analysis

It was late August in 1992, and after a bout of blurred vision that I had accidentally found out was a double vision, I went to an eye doctor who confirmed my vision issues. After several tests that he was able to administer in the office, including various vision tests and even a blood test, Doctor Buonocore scheduled me for an MRI of my brain. He had tested me and ruled out many of the other illnesses with a simple blood test there in the office. I did have to wait a few days for the results of various other tests that the blood test was supposed to reveal, however. When the results came back a few days later, the blood test ruled out cancer as well as other blood-related illnesses, but he wanted to see if an MRI image of my brain would show anything big like a tumor or a growth of some sort. I asked him aside from all those nasty illnesses, was there anything else that it could be, and his response was deadpan.

"Well, it *could* be one other thing, but the chances of you having this would be like you being a New York Yankee with the bases loaded in the bottom of the ninth and down by three runs and you hit a home run to win the game. That is the chances of you having multiple sclerosis."

I felt that this was his way of calming my fears of the unknown in my mind, and for the most part, it worked. I left his office not really concerned.

The MRI tests were easy enough although the claustrophobic effect my mind created was probably a bit extreme for everyone. Although I have never taken an MRI before, being slid into the chamber was a bit surreal. I had to remove any metal as it was a magnet, and I walked into the room. The machine was bigger than I anticipated. The coolness of the room was the second thing that struck me; I was again reminded that once inside the machine, I should not move or move as little as possible. I was given a set of plastic headphones with a local radio station claim and slid into the chamber. Each time that I was forced into the machine, I thought that I would and honestly couldn't go any further, and each time, I was pushed further in. I could feel my heart beating faster and faster; my panic level increasing with every push.

Then suddenly, I came to a stop.

A far-off voice explained that the test will begin shortly. I would feel no pain and would hear only slight harm as the machine worked. As quickly as that, the technician was gone, then the music started playing in the headphones, and the test started.

The test itself was noninvasive and really caused no harm with the exception of the small prick of the injection of the MRI-enhancing solution that was injected halfway through the procedure. After about forty minutes, I was free to leave, and I left with a stress headache.

Several days later, I still had not heard from Doctor Buonocore concerning my situation. After several attempts to contact him by phone the following days, he finally returned my calls at four fifty, Thursday, September 3, 1992. All he told me was that the "MRI showed several lesions on your brain which is consistent with showing in multiple sclerosis."

And just like that, I had hit the home run.

I have to admit that I actually did not know what the illness "multiple sclerosis" was at the time. I had actually thought it was something that Jerry Lewis organized a telethon every year for, but as I found that was MD or muscular dystrophy. Several sentences in the encyclopedia proved my ignorance and fears to be unwarranted and completely wrong. I had never known anyone or anything about multiple sclerosis. I was familiar with Down syndrome as I had grown up with my sister who was a Down syndrome child. I was familiar with cancer as my father had died from Hodgkin's disease when I was six back in 1973, but I had never even heard of multiple sclerosis. In fact, I didn't know anyone who had it.

I was naive, *very* naive.

My world was suddenly in a whirlwind. I picked up every encyclopedia and book having to do with multiple sclerosis that I could find. I spent much of the next few days trying to find every article having to do with multiple sclerosis. Each one said pretty much the exact same thing as far as the illness. There was no cure to date, and each case was different. You can have anywhere from being able to live a normal life showing little to no signs of disability to being completely bedridden, with very extreme cases that can actually cause death in one year. That was extremely rare, however.

At this time, there was no sound reason as to why it was even caused, and there was actually close to having some medicines on the market relatively soon to treat this illness, but again there was no cure. Basically, in every literature I had read, all said the exact same thing…that the common trigger or driving force of the illness appeared to be stress and how it reacts to the body, but that was just the hypothesis that I was seeing in my early readings. Something within the environment could be the trigger, but it was just not known at this time.

To me, the purchasing department and *this* purchasing department in general and how I dealt with it in this atmosphere were extremely stressful for me. I was in the purchasing department for three years, but with that department, there was more than enough stress. I admit that most of the stress was put by myself, but I witnessed several other buyers become purchasing agents be promoted to purchasing agents or even senior purchasing agents! Some were even working a shorter time than I was, yet they were being promoted! I just couldn't understand why I wasn't. Through everything that I was doing in the department, I was still just a "buyer."

I say that because while there were many openings within the department, I found myself getting passed by for all the promotions.

To be a purchasing agent would have been the next step within the department and with it came not only more prestige but more money! It wasn't like a first-come-first-served scenario, so I didn't understand. Due to the salary structure at LILCO, I was not hurting financially, but more was always good. However, the stress of the position and how I perceived it was clearly affecting my health. I had also increased my expenditures substantially rather than saving the money. I felt that I was still living a non-stressful life, but this job was clearly affecting me. Although several people had moved up to a purchasing agent or even a senior purchasing agent, I was continually overlooked. I wanted to receive a substantial raise, and for the first time in my life, *money* had become important to me. Like much of society, I had created a substantial need and wanted to get more money! I was not hurting in any way financially, but like everyone else, I found that I could always use more!

Several positions had opened up within the department, and each time, I was overlooked! Getting to be a purchasing agent or senior buyer would have meant more money to me as well as more prestige or stature. I felt that I had to do something to get myself noticed and more appealing to upper management. I started looking within the company for postings in other departments. Surely, if I put my résumé and to various departments, management would see and understand that I was a valuable commodity! Even if I had no interest in a posted position, I applied for that position. The résumé would go up the line, and management would see it, and they would realize that I would like a raise! Surely, they would see my value and offer me more pay incentives to stay! Each position that I applied for offered at least a $2,500 raise a year to start out with.

Who wouldn't want that?

I got my first interview as a budgeting and cost analyst. I looked at the job before I applied for it, and the description of the position had to do with budgeting money.

"How difficult would that be? I could do that!" I remember saying to myself even though I had absolutely no interest in the budgeting field. I just wanted to be noticed by the management in purchasing.

So I wrote up my application for that position and put it up the chain of command. Again, not truly wanting it but hoping to use it as a weapon to get noticed by my upper management. I was working at the time for a "dictator" so to speak, who was known throughout the entire company as a very difficult person to work for unless you got on his good side. He was a no-nonsense man that was feared throughout the company as a very stern individual and not somebody to mess around with. Everyone within the company that knew of this man would best describe him as a small Italian man with a Napoleon complex. That is to say that although he was great at his job, he was short and really tough! He supposedly was hired to save the purchasing department from the overspending department and the black mark for the company before I got there.

Apparently, that's exactly what he did, but you didn't want to cross him. He had a reputation throughout the company as a very hard and difficult leader but one who got the job done. However, if you did your job correctly, I found him to be extremely nice! I got along great with him, but that was because I think he knew exactly what he was going to get out of me. There was not only some fear that he invoked, but he managed to get respect.

You didn't want to cross him. Within days, the position closed, and I got an interview with Kevin, the manager of Operations Support. I remember walking into the interview not being nervous as I really had nothing to lose, and I didn't really want the job anyway! In fact, I honestly thought that I was just there to make my boss and purchasing department think about what he would be losing if I left. I recall one question that I was asked was if I can handle stress! Aside from laughing to myself and thinking just how stressful numbers could be, my response was simple.

"You know my boss and the reputation he has, I have been there for three years, and I survived."

Everyone knew my boss and the reputation he had, and I used that knowledge to my advantage. I kept on saying that I was not afraid to do anything that was necessary to get the job done, which was sort of the mantra of the purchasing department. That if I was given the tools, I would get the job done correctly and with sufficient knowledge.

A few days later, as I was working on a purchasing issue, it was Karen who came up to me first and congratulated me on getting that position! Within seconds, several other people came to my cubicle offering congratulations. I hadn't heard anything, but apparently, they had.

I got the job!

The position meant an additional $2,500 for me a year, and as I was basically starting to realize that I had become money-hungry, I took the job! Saying goodbye to my friends in the purchasing department was not easy! They threw a party for me and wished me well. I had all the work email addresses and assured them that I would keep in touch with them. Purchasing was an amazing position, and I made a lot of really close friends there as we all shared the common problems of a radical dictatorship department manager. Don't get me wrong, he was really a good guy, but he had a reputation, was a no-nonsense man who ran the department with an iron will...*his* iron will. Anthony had saved the company hundreds of thousands of dollars, and that was important to all the bigwigs in the company. I left with a hug and many good friends.

On my first day at the new position, I was introduced to various people, all of whom gave a warm greeting. The first person I met was Carolyn who was the senior cost analyst. She had short blond hair and was a smartly dressed middle-aged woman. Her desk was the very first cubicle to the left-hand side as I walked into the budgeting department. Of course, there was my new boss Kevin, who was in front of Carolyn's cubicle on the left-hand side of the office. I had already met him at the interview a few weeks prior, so basically, he showed me around. Directly across from their offices was a ten-by-forty-foot area where I was told I'd be sitting with two other people. There was Jeff who was the computer programmer in the department and still another cost analyst named Rob. Within a few hours, I was able to see that Jeff was a very positive individual. He had openly shared with me within hours of meeting him the fact that he had received a kidney transplant a few years ago.

One person in particular, however, I was actually told ahead of time by several people to watch out for by everyone under their breath.

"Oh, did you meet Betty yet?"

I must have been asked that like five times already just walking around the department.

"Who is Betty? I don't think I have" was my response.

Apparently, she had a serious knack for dealing with all her fellow coworkers and had built quite the reputation. I had no idea what they all meant.

"Wait…believe me if you had met her, you would know…"

Betty was a heavyset woman with dyed stringy black hair with some gray streaks as if the dye just didn't adhere to each follicle. She had a booming voice that would let everyone know when she was approaching the room, UNLESS she didn't want to know she was listening! I was told by everyone that I saw that knew she was an issue. From what I heard, she was sweet to your face, but you had to be careful with her. I felt that I had never met anyone that I couldn't handle, so I was not the least bit concerned. LILCO was a union shop, and I've always worked with management as that's what I was. I had dealt with union people in purchasing, so I was not even remotely concerned. She apparently was able to use that status extremely well, though. Almost like a weapon.

I had no idea what that meant.

I believe in unions and what they represent; they definitely serve a purpose, but some people can *use* them negatively. Apparently, that was what was happening here. I was not the least bit concerned as I have always been able to get along with everyone. As I had always felt that I was extremely good-natured and personable to just about everyone, or so I have always been told. I honestly felt I had nothing to worry about. I had never had an issue with anyone, so I took all these warnings with a grain of salt. I guess I would sometimes cross the line with my humor apparently, but as everyone will tell you, I never meant anything by my comments, and I was always just looking for a laugh.

One of my assignments was to organize and see expenditures for only one area of Operations Support. There were monthly accounting reports generated by the computer system that was more of a check and balance of all the numbers. The management would use this to keep track and verify expenditures with visual aids.

That was very confusing for me. As I had no experience at all with statistics and how to track each number and what they meant, I was quickly behind the eight ball. I received little direction other than a brief tutorial, and I quickly sensed the frustration that my boss was having with me.

At this time, I heard in a conversation with Jeff that Betty was actually recently diagnosed with multiple sclerosis also! I told him that I also was recently diagnosed with multiple sclerosis very recently and maybe I should talk with her to show that we had something in common. Surely, it was a way I thought to open the conversation with her and show that we were on the same page. I approached her from behind and basically started the conversation with her.

"Got a few seconds to talk, Betty?" I asked.

She turned quickly and pleasantly responded, "Sure, Peter. What's on your mind?"

Maybe I had no business broaching the subject at all, but it just blurted out, "We have a lot in common, the two of us. I was diagnosed with multiple sclerosis not too long ago, and I hear you were also."

I never truly anticipated that someone would be very uncomfortable sharing this information so freely and certainly not with a person that she worked with. I mean, I was overly open about the illness, and I thought everyone was!

She was obviously taken aback.

I was intrigued with someone who had knowledge or experience with what I was exactly dealing with, and I wanted to see what her feelings were on that. I never anticipated that anyone would have a negative reaction, but I guess I understood. Basically, I was a total stranger approaching her on her new diagnosis, and she didn't know me from a hole in the head. I walked out of the cubicle, and I felt as if

I had intruded on her, but I hope she felt okay with me. I understood what she would do, and hopefully she understood my situation.

One of the position assignments was that I was put in charge of putting together a weekly report that basically explained the numbers in visual graphs, printing them up, and bringing the copies to all the upper management. As silly as it may sound, I was able to show some creativity which I have always enjoyed, making these charts. There was no creativity involved in it, but I was able to draw with a computer program that I had never used before! It was a program called Harvard Graphics. There was a bit of a learning curve that I had to go through, but I was able to gradually improve the quality of the graphics each week. I'm not sure if anybody even noticed, but it made me very happy! I looked to print these reports each week and distribute them among upper management. I did not know how the numbers were created to an extent or what the numbers meant, but I liked to create the reports and hand them out to upper management.

I felt pretty good at this point that the job; however, I did miss my friends in purchasing. Once a month, I was able to organize a luncheon with everyone that I used to work with, and we would meet in a restaurant in between the purchasing department at 445 Broadhollow Road in Melville and my new position in Operations Support at 175 E. Old Country Road in Hicksville for lunch. That became a highlight to me as I was able to creatively write to the people in purchasing about the lunch we all had.

Because the table at the restaurant was long, many conversations would get unheard, so I created a journal, and I emailed to the people in purchasing called "My Side of the Table." I wrote about in silly detail what everyone had ordered for lunch and the conversations that pursued at the meal. I had no interest or ability to be in the budgeting department; and apparently my new boss, had given up trying to teach me! He really had no clue how to be a successful manager and to deal with uncontrolled situations that didn't go his way. I honestly felt that I was doing my best. Apparently, I wasn't what he expected, and he was not adept at training anyone to do any different.

I got into trouble one day simply minding my own business when I was facing my computer doing some cost analyst work that I was supposed to know what I was doing. I was sitting with my back to the conversation, minding my own business. Mark, a short, gray-bearded man from upper management, strolled in and was having a conversation with anyone that could hear. He was talking about something that happened in his house, and he was telling everybody about it.

"Well, there was a window at the top of the shelf and was letting in all kinds of rain and moisture into the room!" Mark continued, "It was causing a lot of molds on the walls!"

Suddenly, Betty chimed in, "I would have to hire somebody to close the window because I wouldn't be able to reach it!

Mark was quick and spouted out, "That is because you're vertically challenged." He was referring to her height.

I spun around in my chair and laughed out loud! I had never heard that before!

"Vertically challenged! How funny is that?" I rolled my chair back, shaking my head!

Apparently, Betty was not amused, and I was told that she ran into the bathroom crying.

After several other people went into the bathroom to see what had happened, I was called into upper management and told that Betty was deeply hurt by my laughter and wanted to press charges against me!

Mind you, I didn't say a word, but *I just laughed at what Mark had said!*

I just laughed!

Nothing was said to Mark because he just apologized, but the company was threatened with a lawsuit just because I laughed at what was said! Management once again settled with Betty and told her that they would handle it. That seemed to make her happy. Once again, the company had caved to this woman! I believe that this woman had used the system and had gotten her way six times already and was not to be pushed around. The result for me was I was sort of banished! I had my seat changed where I was put in a small four-by-four cubicle all by myself instead of getting what little education and direction or help with anything that I didn't understand regarding that cost-analyst position! The fact that she was able to make the company bigwigs succumb to her whims apparently never really escaped her. She continued to use the system because the company allowed her to!

An example of this was I was having a conversation with Jeff, who had become a housing repair contractor on the side for a business that he was starting. We were just having a private conversation. He described one of the operations for a construction job he was performing called "fenestration." I had no idea what that was, but anyone in construction would know it as the arrangement of windows and doors on the elevation of the building. He said that he needed a window in a wall that allows the passage of light in.

Any contractor would know about this and really not be offended by it as there was nothing to be offended by, but a person mistakenly eavesdropping and looking for something to press charges on anything would hear something different!

Unfortunately, Miss Betty misheard the phrase "fenestration" as "penetration." Since she didn't know what it was, she had to be offended by it. She quickly ran into the Operations Support upper-management office in tears and threatened that she was going to see a lawyer and press charges on Jeff and me for talking about "sexual penetration."

Before we knew it, Jeff and I were both called into the Operations Support's general manager Manfred office, and the door was closed firmly behind us to explain ourselves. We sat there as Manfred told us what the complaint was, and Jeff and I both just shook our heads. Jeff explained what "fenestration" was and how it was used in his contracting business. It can be defined as an opening in the wall, door, roof, or vehicle that allows the passage of light and may also allow the passage of sound and sometimes air. She was eavesdropping where she shouldn't have been and got offended at something she didn't know what it was! She did not even come close to hearing what was said and knew she had to be offended.

Manfred just shock his head.

Jeff and I agreed that this woman was trouble, but the damage was already done.

CHAPTER 19

A New Band

TOMMY, RICHIE, AND I GOT together in the spring of 1993 like we always had done in years past. We sat down at the Terrace diner on the corner of Sunrise Highway and Belmont Avenue by my mom's house. We usually met there to discuss "band discussions." We met there that night on Thursday, April 13, 1995, to discuss our plans for the band. We hadn't played together since the gig at Spring Fest 1992 at the Nassau Center in Woodbury. That was a good gig, but like every gig that we had played since our inception of playing together, at the end of the gig, we all wanted to get away from each other. We played really good music together, but we each got on each other's nerves! Plus, we all had our own lives that didn't respond well to each other *if* we didn't have a gig to play. I know that I myself had very little time to do anything that could take up a lot of time! (I was a manager of a Little League team and I was responsible to set up and run our softball team), I had *little time*. Don't get me wrong, *if* I wanted it bad enough, I would find the time to do whatever I wanted. I also would spend some time with Cathi. It all seemed to work, believe it or not!

Tommy had picked up Richie, so I knew the meeting would take place. I loved Richie, but he had a habit of making a promise and just not showing up or canceling at the last minute. So Tommy getting him was the best guarantee that he would get there! I walked in and was totally happy to see these guys. It had been too long. It was good to see these guys. After a few minutes of overall silliness, we agreed that we all wanted to play together again. We spoke about what we all wanted to do and what was needed. We all liked the fact of having a singer, but we had never tried a female singer. We agreed that this would open up a great amount of freedom and ultimately change our sound.

Cathi and I were just sort of dating again but not really committed to each other after what we had just gone through. I still didn't know what happened, and I guess I never really wanted to either. I was going slowly with her; to be honest, I was actually eliminating various memories or just plain not putting one and one together. Conrad had joined the Navy, I think. Sometimes, I thought about that situation, and I was still living in denial about it. Mostly, we just never spoke about it. I had *literally forgotten* that I had walked out on her on Christmas Eve! *I swear!* I had even convinced myself that maybe they had just slept together just one time. That still wouldn't have been all right with me, but that was a bit better to swallow. Once, she actually said, in what I thought of was a slip of the tongue, that she had dated *someone* for like four months, but I never really put the pieces together. I was with Colleen anyway.

During a night out with Cathi, I mentioned in conversation that we might be looking for a female singer for the band. Cathi said that Ruth, a girl that I had met a few times and whom she worked with, could sing and wanted to be in a band again. I didn't know Ruth could sing, and I felt that it would be a great idea to ask her if she was interested. I spoke to the guys, and they were all on board with having her come down to practice, just to see how it would go.

I asked Cathi to give her my number so I could set everything up. I told Ruth how to get to the practice and when it would be. We have practiced at my mother's house, in the basement for years, and this would be no different. My mother was beyond awesome in that she would let me practice in the basement anytime that I wanted. That was beyond awesome! I guess she would rather have me at home *safe* than partying all hours of the night! My sister's bedroom was right above the drum set also! That was why I would get annoyed if we went over ten! My mother was so great! I could never forget that!

I introduced Ruth to the guys, and she fit right in. She had dark brown wavy hair that gave a hint of being parted in the middle. She wasn't wearing a lot of makeup and was almost natural-looking. And she wore a blue checkerboard flannel shirt. By checkerboard, I mean to say that there were two or three different shades of blues ranging from light blues to dark blue and even blacks in little one-by-one-inch boxes. Her sleeves were rolled up on each arm to the elbow, and she wore basic dark blue jeans.

Pauli joined us to play drums that night once again. He was the drummer we had when we had played the second Spring Fest show in 1992. As I had said, he kept decent time, and he was available! We didn't want to audition a drummer; we just wanted to see what Ruth could bring to the table!

We played our usual set of songs—"I Saw Her Standing There" by the Beatles, "You Got Me Where You Want Me" by the Romantics—just basic stuff to see how she would fit in, and she had a decent voice! We had learned a Jewel song "Standing Still," "Everywhere to Me" by Michelle Branch, and she sounded great! A bonus was that she harmonized well also! She had asked me on the phone days ago if we knew "Respect," which Aretha Franklin made famous, so I had the boys learn that! We went through that four or five times, and it was obvious that she could sing! We sounded pretty good as a band! I think she was a good fit. I felt very comfortable with her, and I knew that we all did. Having a girl in the band was something that I never thought I would have. Not because it was wrong, or whatever, but because I just never had thought that we needed one. I only played in a band with a female singer for one situation back in 1985. That show ended up being a strange evening with me spending time with the female singer after the show.

I thought I actually sensed some unmistakable flirting going on between Ruth and me though! A look here and a smile there; I wasn't imagining this. I don't think I was anyway. Practice went well, but I thought I would just ask Ruth if she wanted to get together just to go over a couple of things. Maybe we could meet and work some things out. Maybe even have dinner?

"Do you think that maybe I could come by just to go over a few songs?"

Ruth jumped at the idea. "I was just going to ask you the same thing! How about Friday night?"

And just like that, we had plans to meet up and go over a few songs.

I showed up at her apartment promptly at six that April 21, 1995.

I parked in the driveway right behind her dirty white Chevrolet Caprice that was more than a few years old. It had a blue interior, which was very similar to my mother's Oldsmobile Cutlass Sierra which she seemed to have forever. Actually, my mom had the very same interior! Except my mom's front seat had puffed wheat all over the interior because my sister ate in the car on the way to work every morning…but that is another story!

I walked around back as she had instructed me to do, and the stairs were right there as she had said. I walked down the stairs, a cement stairway with rubber treads covering them to make it relatively safe, and I knocked on the door of her basement apartment. She opened the door right away, and I was honestly surprised that she kissed me on the cheek. We had never done that, but whatever.

"Thanks for coming over," she said.

"No problem." I said.

She was dressed casually in jeans and a black T-shirt from a Heart concert which she had apparently seen.

"I hope you're hungry, I figured we'd eat first, okay? I made some pasta. The sauce is a jar sauce, but it is pretty good. You want a beer? Or I have some red wine… I have both. What do you want?"

And within seconds, we were both sitting at her table sipping the wine.

I never expected this. Then again, I didn't know what to expect. She was really in control here.

"What songs give you the most issues here?" I figured I would ask.

She poured herself a glass of wine and had a sip.

Several glasses of wine later, we finished one bottle, and the pasta dinner was consumed; I was feeling very good. So much so that the conversation wasn't on music at all when we finally kissed. She kissed really well, and we were hot and heavy for about ten minutes or so when she suddenly rose up and headed for her bedroom.

"Wait!" I said. "I don't have anything…"

She put my nerves to rest, almost instantly.

"We are not doing that!"

"Oh, of course not…" I said, feeling almost embarrassed.

She took my hand and led me to the bed where we spent the next few hours just exploring each other. Somewhere in the evening, we must have fallen asleep for the next thing I knew, light was streaming into the downstairs apartment.

It was morning.

CHAPTER 20

"Little" Issues

CATHI AND I WERE DATING exclusively again, but things had definitely changed in my mind. I was having a really hard time understanding or even remembering things and what had happened. I honestly didn't remember anything that had happened between us. I blacked out, memory wise, for that entire time. If anyone asked me what had happened the last few months, I honestly didn't know. I guess all that really mattered was Cathi and I were back together. My opinions about her had actually changed, however. Where I was very close to committing to spending the rest of my life with her, I had a daily dark feeling that this situation would be only temporary. I didn't trust her, and it would have taken me a long time to get back to that, *if ever*.

Gone was the overall urgency of tying the knot with her. I had once had the dream of waiting at the end of the aisle for her as she walked down the church aisle dressed in her wedding dress on her father's arm. I couldn't see that anymore. I didn't trust her, and without trust, there was nothing. We dated for another few years, and I just couldn't rely on the feelings that I had. Her life was also being turned upside down, and I was just going for the ride with her.

Her mother and father had gotten a divorce, and her father was getting remarried. I never spoke with her about how this was affecting her, but I am sure it must have been tough. When I spoke to Cathi about this, all she would say was she was fine and would call her new mother-in-law a *monster-in-law*. Cathi's mom and her entire family had actually been invited to her dad's and the new mother-in-law's wedding reception! Talk about an awkward moment! Cathi and I went to the wedding, and she wore a beautiful tight red dress. I was getting really jealous because everyone was looking at her. I honestly think Cathi wanted it! I mean, who wouldn't want to be noticed? Cathi was very attractive as I had mentioned before, and that was why I got really annoyed when she was talking with the DJ for some time, and he ended up playing "Lady in Red" by Chris De Burgh. That was a *clear* flirt! She also spent a good portion of the wedding singing "La Bamba," which was a *direct dig* at Colleen because of her heritage. I think she was part Puerto Rican or Mexican, or whatever she was—I am not even sure what she was, never even noticed and frankly didn't really care—but it was really starting to piss me off!

A few weeks later, her younger sister had got engaged and was set to be married. This was probably too much for Cathi. In her mind, *she* was supposed to be married first, but I wanted none of that. It was soon after that time that Cathi broke up with me. We had lasted eight years together: four years ago when I thought about marrying her and before the entire *dick* Conrad thing and I broke with her on Christmas Eve because of him, and the four years now. I really couldn't blame her for the recent four years. Conrad had ruined everything for me. I was just enjoying myself, and I just couldn't drum up the desire to marry her anymore.

CHAPTER 21

It Gets Worse

I STARTED KEEPING A JOURNAL of all the wrongs that this department; Betty, Kevin, and Manfred in general were putting me through daily. I was there in the department for just about three years, and while I left the purchasing department three years ago for money and the promise of better situations, but I had yet to receive a decent evaluation to warrant any increase and nothing for two and a half years to my salary. Almost *three years*, and I hadn't received a penny increase! Actually, that was not really true. Kevin had authorized the department to put me on probation within the first four months. I was scheduled to have my yearly review, but that never happened! I was put on *probation* and given only and extra $1,000 on my yearly salary and told that I wasn't living up to why I was hired! No extra training, just I was told that I was on *probation*! I looked this up in the company "Rules and Regulations," and I could be let go!

The review was supposed to be for a year, but I was only in the department for four months at the time. Apparently, I wasn't doing the job to what he thought was acceptable! Never mind trying to help me learn the job better, he felt it necessary to put me on "probation" and punish me that way as opposed to helping me and teaching me!

I questioned him at this review about why this would be like this, and he told me, "That is why I had to not give you a full raise and place you on probation. Your work is subpar."

Thus increased my nightmare! My wonderful boss, Kevin, didn't communicate at all with me, and each time my evaluation was due, for some reason or another, it just never happened! That was my fault as I just hid and did not make a big deal of it because I was scared! Every day I was scared that I was going to be let go, and so I never really put up a fight about it! I honestly believed that I had gone under the radar so speak. I just existed, and nobody had to keep tabs on me. However, I took myself in and went once a week or so to speak with human resources about my situation.

Wilhelmina was the person in human resources that I spoke with. I sat in her office, and we basically spoke about what was happening. I would go into her office maybe once a week just to talk. I looked forward to sitting with her as she became a voice of reason in this situation. One day, she was looking a little down, and she confided in me that she had just lost her father recently. We just sat in her office tearing up together as she spoke openly about him to me.

After telling her my situation, I really feel like we kind of built an understanding. She started to listen to what I was saying and actually started to hear me. I told her about the journal I had written about how I was being treated in Operations Support, Kevin, Manfred, and Betty. At this time, *my* journal was forty-two pages of Times New Roman font of twelve font size. The words highlighting everything that was said and done in a negative fashion to me. I wrote about my situation: from the lack of direction of handling my employment in the department, from Kevin, and the lack of direction from Manfred to the totally inappropriate situation with Betty, and how it ruined me—to the lack of a proper evaluation for three years now, and how I seemed to fall through the cracks within that department. I presented to her a copy of the forty-two-page and growing daily journal that I was writing each day as something happened for her to read. I left the copy with her.

Ultimately, I was told that there was a personality conflict between myself and Kevin and that I would be transferred to another position. Mind you, I never had a personality conflict with anyone *ever*, but I agreed simply because it would be better for me in the long run.

After work one day, my friend, Jennifer, was leaving the office, and my car was right behind hers. Jennifer and I had been friends in the purchasing department a few years back, and she had left purchasing a while back like I did. We would go downstairs just about once a week to have frozen yogurt in the 445 building together. I laughed as I followed her car onto Old Country Road where she made a left at the light. I waved at her goodbye and drove through the red light. She managed to make the left as the light changed and never saw me barrel into a car that was just leaving the LILCO/Market Span/Key Span parking lot! I slammed on the breaks but still felt my car slam into a fellow Keyspan car and crumble under mine. The image of him falling in the car front seat will forever haunt me.

I thought I had killed him!

It was across the street at the corner from the medical center for LILCO at 100 Old Country Road in Hicksville. When the cars first met at the intersection, several nurses ran out from the medical center. I blamed the falling sunset that was directly in a rearview mirror for obscuring my vision, but it was just my negligence and lack of paying attention that caused it.

Jennifer didn't even see me wave to her, and she swore that she had never even seen me. The result was that another car of mine was now deemed inoperable and had to be towed. Luckily, the man was not hurt, and when the police report was written, I said that it was "All my fault," saying that the sun had blinded my vision. I said that I just couldn't see the light had changed. Obviously, that was not true, but what else could I have said?

The next morning, my insurance policy had supplied me with a car, and I was able to get to work. My car would once again be fixed, and my rates would jump again!

Wilhelmina ultimately agreed with me and spoke to the department management and arranged that I would be transferred out and given another position. Apparently, it was proven and said that I had a personality conflict with Kevin and that it was detrimental.

I was given a schedule analyst position, of which I would organize outside contractors, work on permits, and arrange different contractors for work that had been done in the field.

Once again, I had completely no idea what this was about, and I was unqualified for the position! This time I was to schedule people and contractors to do different electrical construction. I was given some training, but I just couldn't comprehend it and had to schedule contractors for various jobs. That position lasted only six months as I once again had to rely on other people to do my job! I was clearly not qualified for the position as my lack of electrical and construction knowledge limited me. The stress was absolutely intolerable!

The company that I was working for was going through various mergers, and they were constantly changing the name. On December 30, 1996, the Long Island Lighting Company merged with Brooklyn Union Gas and became Marketspan, a company that would supply both electricity and gas for all of Long Island. That only lasted for only six weeks, and the company was bought out and became Keyspan, a company that would sell natural gas and electric retail and wholesale.

All this meant was I was cast in limbo!

Before the end of the year, I was transmitted to the real estate department within the now new company, Keyspan. I had to learn another job that had to deal with all the real estate properties that the company owned on Long Island. I had to learn all the permits that we needed some work to be done! The only good thing was I was placed in a cubicle right near the purchasing department! The purchasing department had gone through its own share of changes since I was gone the three years. They didn't negotiate price anymore, which was a staple of the purchasing department; they had implemented a computer program that they had started when I first left. They had a new manager as Anthony the manager was in charge when I was there had been asked to leave…or fired.

Within a few months of working in the real estate department, although I thought I was doing an okay job, I couldn't really do what was needed to be done there either. Despite any sort of direction, I was banished (I felt anyway) to a four-by-four cubicle directly in between the purchasing department and the real estate department where I was told to shred documents for eight hours a day! The department had a tremendous number of documents that had to be shredded, and not having anything to do with anything, apparently, they found the need to do that!

I had become a glorified document shredder! That was what my five years of college education had brought me! I was making the *exact* amount a year that I had been making since I was screwed out of a decent raise by Kevin in Operation Support three years ago and counting now!

I had fallen through the cracks of the company going through various mergers, and there was no place for me. Every day I would look within the company want ads to see what positions were now available. That was also very difficult because the company had merged two companies together, and there was a downsizing of various departments as the new company developed. The upper management of this huge company had vowed to everyone here that "Absolutely no layoffs would happen, and everyone would find a new home within the company walls"! You couldn't have one company in Brooklyn and one on Long Island both doing the same thing!

There were several moments of the bigwigs trying to figure out and having to eliminate the overlap with the merging company. It had been four years since I had received my last financial raise, and because I had moved around so much within the company, nobody would step up and do my review! With the two companies merging together, there were a lot of positions that had to be filled and would ultimately need to be eliminated if they were duplicated with the two companies merging. There were a few positions that were posted on the internal company listing, but I knew I had to find something for myself. There were several positions that I applied to. I was actually told that I couldn't apply to them as they didn't have a record that I even existed within the company! Therefore, I had to do my own evaluation if I want to apply for a job!

Give me a break!

I filled out my own evaluation and gave it to human resources. Believe me, I was tougher than most people would have been on myself! I told them that I was a slow learner, but once I was given proper direction and instructions, I was a very good employee! However, shocks of shocks, I still did not get a raise! I mean let's face it; there was nobody better at shredding paper than I was! However, I was marked as a satisfactory employee and allowed to apply for any job that I wanted within the company! I applied for just one though. It was a job as a marketing specialist within the company. I had at the very least years ago found this interesting.

I applied for the job and ultimately got it.

However, I knew I was in over my head. Although I thought at one time I could have easily done this job, I felt like I was once again lost in what I was expected to do! I felt that I was dealing with a lot of fatigue daily, no matter how much I slept at night, but especially after lunch. Everyone has that, but I was actually finding it happening regularly now.

When I was in Operations Support, I actually would go into a stall in the bathroom and rest for a time! For the past few months, I had actually been falling asleep, be it in my car or, yes, sometimes even at my desk. I actually had mastered putting my leg up and appearing to be looking at the computer screen. There was nothing I could do to fight this off! I actually had clocked myself in and fell asleep at my desk as weeks went by for a record of fourteen minutes! I would go into the bathroom and close the door in a stall; I just couldn't keep my eyes open.

Nobody would be proud of this, but it was what it was.

One meeting after lunch, I was called into a meeting with everyone in my "new" department. It was a meeting that I was being told things that I should have been able to follow. As everything that was being said to me really didn't really interest me enough to keep me focused, I was having problems keeping my eyes open. My new "boss of the day" took me aside after the meeting and asked me what was wrong.

"I saw you falling asleep in there," he said. "Is everything all right? What's wrong?"

I couldn't do this anymore. I had gone full out for a number of years, and I couldn't do this anymore. It was over.

"I have multiple sclerosis."

To his credit, I was told to see the company doctor that day, and I was sent home. That company doctor was more or less a waste, but

I guess he had to earn his salary somehow. He didn't know what to do and sent me home for some "rest."

I took it as a sign, and I "retired" that day, November 11, 1998, never to work again!

CHAPTER 22

My "Real Friends"

WHILE EVERYTHING WAS GOING ON with Conrad and Cathi, I received still another bad sign from one of my "so-called" friends. This friend whom I had hung out with for many years and organized various get-togethers since our days at Caldor, I have played cards with, drank much beer with, have been hanging out with for a few years now, went on double dates with him and his girlfriend, even went up to his house upstate in the snow a few years ago, and I had included in just about everything that I had organized, and we were the very first to hang out with him when he returned from the Navy. My "friend" Bert also made a pass at my girlfriend, Cathi, while I was screaming about Conrad. Worse than that, it was premeditated! He had told a few of the guys that we all hung out with, part of the group that I played cards with, Dungeons & Dragons with, and hung out with that he was going to do this! They all expressed shock and basically told him *not to do it*!

He still tried.

He had heard my situation with Conrad and decided that he would take it upon himself to actually think that this was a good time to make a pass at Cathi! He then tried to kiss her. After he was rejected by Cathi and I ultimately found out about it, I guess he panicked and tried to explain himself. He ended up leaving a rather lengthy message on my answering machine when I found out about it. Never once did he apologize or say that he was wrong to do it, but he just rambled on about some mistake that really made no sense. He closed the conversation on the answering machine that day after rambling about what had happened with a silly Navy proverb that he had learned in all his years in the Navy and used it to explain his actions.

"You know they can teach you one thousand ways to kill a human…so let me know."

What did that mean? He closed with those exact words. Never once did he apologize for the total disregard of trust and our friendship. Needless to say, I never called him back. This situation with Cathi opened up a lot of the eyes to me in terms of what real friendship is all about. I am humbled to know that those other friends whom I had hung out with, played all those games with, and hung out with drinking or played Dungeons & Dragons and cards with didn't hang out with him either.

That is what true friendship is.

EPILOGUE

As of September 3, 2022, I have now had multiple sclerosis for thirty years. *Thirty years!* I firmly believe, now more than ever, that everything that happened to me, even to this day, was because of the stress level that I was given at the time. There were many outside influences, *many* that I had no control over, and it affected me poorly! I know that there was a great deal of stress in my life brought on by others as you have read here.

Stress is a state of mental or emotional strain or tension resulting from adverse or very demanding circumstances. After reading this book, can you see and understand why this affected me? Now I am not smart enough to know what actually causes this illness, be it environmental, chemical, or even as some are saying hereditary or maybe something else, but I do know what causes it to run rapid in your life. I don't think in my case it was hereditary as I am the only one in my family history (that I know) that has ever had this, but I do know what exasperated it. What was the "fuel to the fire" so to speak?

In most situations, stress and how your body is beaten down by it is such a horrible thing, if not controlled. I think that everyone that has been diagnosed with multiple sclerosis can go back to the very time in their life when they were diagnosed with this and see that they were dealing with an absorbent amount of stress. That is just my theory though, but stress is not the only thing that causes this illness. Far from it! But it definitely exasperated it, and in my case, it definitely added to it. In layman's terms, the illness finds a "kink in the armor" (so to speak) and exploits itself. I was under a great amount of stress for a very long time. Some caused by myself, I admit, but mostly caused by external issues as I have shown you.

I am not saying that stress is the only thing that causes this illness, far from it, but it definitely is the common factor. Everyone has stress, and everyone reacts to it differently. Once you have that "kink in the armor," and I am not saying *how* you got it, it can grow and grow and grow. It is like a cancer! The prolonged and unwanted stress that I didn't deserve, and couldn't deal with, was more than I could bear. In my case, it was a series of events that contributed to my downfall. Who knows if it would have surfaced if my life had been different. Would this illness have been in my life if I didn't have all the stress that was forced on me? Everyone has stress, that's why it is important to learn how to control it, manipulate it, and use it to your benefit. Find a place where you can just close your eyes and just breathe or meditate. I feel so much better when I take a few minutes to just breathe. I take some time DAILY just to meditate. There are a *lot* of places or programs where for no or little money down you can learn to meditate. Find a few minutes to breathe for yourself.

I will let you judge for yourself what weakened my armor so to speak. In hindsight, I think it is very easy for me to see what caused me so much stress, but I am not going to rehash it now. After all, I have done that this entire book. Everything written here is honest and truthful and happened just the way it is written here! I am in a better place mentally today, and while it was difficult for me to write this book and look back, I can once and for all put the issues to rest.

As I said, I am happy, and I am content with where I am in my life today.

I think that if I blame stuff in my past, I must also *thank stuff from my past for this*. Today, I am doing very well! I am not bitter any-more. I am happy, and I have lived a *great* life! Yes, there were bumps in the road, but what life is perfect?

I have met some absolutely amazing people because of this ill-ness and where I am today. You should always remember that mul-tiple sclerosis is not the end of it all but rather it can be a beginning. Let it be the beginning for you and move forward, *not* back!

I truly believe that everything in my thirty years was cause and effect.

And this is how *my* stress impacted my thirty-year journey with *multiple sclerosis*.

A WAVE OF EMOTION

I'm in the middle of Orion's belt, high above her looking down.
It's the fourteenth day of the month of March, and I stand at an angle
    without a sound.
She say's "I'm here for you and you are for me, or is that so hard to
    see?"
And I see the eyes of surrender as "I" now becomes "we."
I'm on the shores of "Lake Copiague," with my back against the sand.
We both fall hard, together as one, but it's me who loses who I am.
She says, "When we get married, there will be no one else around."
And I see with the eyes of the child as we start to settle down.
And it comes on like a wave, wave on the ocean.
And howls like the wind, a wind of erosion.
    And it drives like the rain…
    It comes on like a wave, a wave of emotion.
I'm sitting on the porch up at Tommy's house, counting "peddidles"
    by hand.
The whole gang is there playing musical chairs, and it's you who
    wants us to be the last to stand.
She says, "Never color your eyes green 'cause sooner or later, you'll
    always see red."
And she uses the word "friendship" like a veil to hide her head.
    He says "I'll be here to lean on, but I'll never hold you up."
    For this is just my body, and my blood is in this cup.
    "We are not responsible for lies beneath the sheets…
I am the voice of reason; you are valid in your needs!"

I am lost on the trails up at "Sawyer Island"; there's a whole new
    world in which to roam.
But every day away, it's just another day in which where one day close
    to home.
She says, "I'm not to blame… I would never dial the phone!"
And I'm blurred with the eyes of faith as you wait for the dial tone.
Falling down a spiral staircase, high above her looking down…
It's the very first day of a brand-new year as my love for her finally
    hits the ground.
She says, "You have to stand Pat, forgive, Forget and carry on!"
And I watch with the eyes of a stranger as you fell into the arms of
    a friend.

Peter J. Licari, 2/1992

THE WALLS JUST
DON'T GO UP HIGH ENOUGH

Her nose is keen, and she thinks smells a rat as she prances around
her garbage.
She has powerful ears that picked up every sound, and she makes up
what she doesn't hear to make it all work.
She doesn't care whose back she stands on, using the system to help
justify her needs.
You see she fancies herself a Christian, but those who know her see
her true ambition.
With a double-edged sword, she sets the double meaning to the
double standard…
She lets everyone know just what everyone is saying every
moment of the day.
The walls just don't go up high enough.
And she gulps at the wine that nobody has offered.
On her shelves, she keeps many objects to protect her.
Tiny plastic trinkets she believes show her faith.
She whispers a lot but lets you know what she's saying,
and never pays attention to those who don't care what she has to say.
For she hides behind her interpretation of the good book,
believing that she is a protector of all; she pushes them hard until
they fall.
Hiding behind the Bible, she rests on the fray,
Attacking the weakest member for what he didn't say.
One by one, she takes them all to her payday…

But the company created her, and so they have no one to blame
    anyway.
With a booming voice, she lets us all hear what she wants us to hear…
And she plays her cards like a master.
She's good at making everything her business then gets furious at
    what she thinks she hears!
She uses the system in plays the Savior…
But do you really think He really approves of your behavior?

September 10, 2010

ABOUT THE AUTHOR

PETER J. LICARI WAS DIAGNOSED with Multiple Sclerosis 30 years ago on September 3, 1992, but that didn't stop him! He has written 3 books, recorded 2 CDs with his band (NORTH), was a stand-up comic for 2 shows, had a public access TV show for two months which he wrote, directed, edited and stared in with several of his friends. Peter is the proud father of a son studying music education at college!

www.ingramcontent.com/pod-product-compliance
Lightning Source LLC
Chambersburg PA
CBHW070834160726
48004CB00001B/371